TEACHING CHILDREN TO RIDE PONIES

Teaching Children to Ride Ponies

Chapter 1 Before we Begin

- Choosing the right Pony
- Tack and Equipment
- Clothing for the Rider
- Facilities required
- Duration of lessons
- Where to Ride
- Qualities of the Children's Instructor

Chapter 2 Introduction to Riding

- The Beginning
- First Lesson
- Lesson 2
- Lesson 3
- Lesson 4
- Subsequent Lessons
- When to come off the Lead rein

Chapter 3 Having Fun on Ponies

- Bringing fun into riding
- Games to Play
- Suggested Races
- Exercises
- Handy Pony
- Hacking Out with Ponies

Chapter 4 Stable Management

- When and where to Teach Stable management
- Early lessons
- Written work for the child

Chapter 5 Advancing the Child Rider

- The Canter
- Trotting Poles
- Jumping
- Use of school movements
- Riding in open areas

Chapter 6 The future

- The pony Club
- The Chosen Disciplines
- Mock Shows
- The First Show

Chapter 7 Giving Something Back to your Pony Especially for the kids

- Listening to what the pony has to say
- Signs of pain to look for
- Massage and Touch
- Why Massage?

- How do I massage my Pony?
- How long do I Massage my Pony?

Dedication

I dedicate this book to my wonderful horses and ponies. They have made my life so very special. Lady, my first horse, who I was given by my beloved mum when I was eighteen years old. Lady gave me a daughter a son and a granddaughter. She was a very special horse who gave me and my family so much joy. Dancer and Merry who taught so many young children the joys of horsemanship. Such kind natured, gentle ponies. Jack, who taught children how to sit a rearing pony and survive. A little chap who came to me after suffering abuse at the hands of someone who thought brute force would sort out his behaviour problems. Jaffar, a horse for any day of the week. Jaffar calms my soul and takes me on heavenly hacks around my home. She reads my mind and feeds my soul. We gallop over the fields and I feel like a child again. Bella, the horse that demands respect from me and all who ride her. Respect her or find yourself face down in the middle of the field! A lovely horse ,who teaches people to understand the complexity of the equine spirit. Betty, a dear old mare that looks after the novice and nervous riders. She makes everyone feel so happy. Prince, the pony that gives little girls their first crush. Another complex character who will suffer no fools. Velvet, the little pony given away free with a house. I was so lucky to have her passed to me. She takes the little tiny tots on their first horseback adventures. A sweet, obliging little pony with a kind heart. Henry, a big hunk of a horse that loves to keep a harem of mares who take up all his time. A cheeky but charming boy who is so very handsome. Rosie and her wonderful daughter, Angel, two naughty girls who laugh at us humans as we try to tame their wild traveller spirit. My special gypsy cobs that make me proud as they dance and prance around the fields. Dusty, saved from a life of pain and anguish. A naughty girl but beautiful enough to get away with it. Peanut, the king of the horse world. Makes young girls go week at the knees, and old girls too. Moss, a gentle and kind spirit that tries always to please his rider. Yet another ladies man and so handsome to boot.

My horses, my life.

Introduction

Teaching Children to Ride Ponies is an intended guide for, not only riding instructors, but also parents and relatives who wish to teach their own children to ride. The parents and instructor could actually work together, so long as they go at the same rate. The parent must not be tempted to hurry the process if they feel the instructor is going to slowly.

The guide has been written as simply as possible and all technical jargon has been kept to a minimum. This book is written in down to earth language that everyone should be able to understand.

Having taught children to ride for over thirty years I, the author, have the experience of the years to share with the reader. Some of my views may not be conventional but the back up of my experience makes sure I know what I am rambling about.

The book also considers the mother, father, and aunts, uncles etc who are just ordinary folk like me. No massive income, no dashing to the saddle shop on a whim to buy various aids. This is why I have suggested some homemade articles such as the Daisy Rein.

I have loved horses and ponies all my life and there was never a time when I was not thinking and dreaming of them. I have read all there is to read and I have studied endlessly. I gained my British Horse Society certificates and also went to university to take part in Equine Studies. I left with my Bachelor of Science in the subject and still continue to study to this very day.

I have written, what I consider, some delightful animal stories which your children may also enjoy. These can be purchased from Amazon and are available in paperback and in Kindle format. All my stories are enjoyed by young and old alike.

I sincerely hope you enjoy reading the book as much as I have enjoyed writing it.

Teaching Children to Ride Ponies

Chapter 1 Before we Begin

When a child places their foot on the first rung of the riding ladder it is vital to get it right. It is your job as an instructor to protect the child as much as is humanly possible. Although falling off is an integral part of learning to ride, the first fall must be avoided for as long as possible. Falls will happen, they are inevitable. However, the longer we can avoid them, the better the foundations will be. If falls start too early confidence could be dented beyond repair.

Falls are unfortunately unavoidable during a riding career. No matter how hard the instructor tries to avoid a rider falling. The unexpected does happen. If you have done your best and a fall takes place then you must not feel bad about it. The pony has a mind of its own and can only be controlled to a certain degree. Horses and ponies are predictable to a certain extent, however there is always a possibility that the unexpected can happen. During early riding careers, if all safety rules are followed, falls are usually of a minor nature. In the present climate of health and safety etc, some parents think that their child must never fall off! A child I was teaching many years ago took a tumble. The following week her mum requested that her daughter should not fall off again. I very politely pointed out that I could never guarantee this. I also suggested she found another riding teacher as I could not provide what she requested. Rules to assist in avoiding injury are as follows:

- Hard riding hats must be worn at all times, even for grooming and fetching in from pasture
- Boots with a heel

- Long sleeved tops
- Neck straps on the pony
- Safety stirrups
- Lead rein when necessary
- Riding in an enclosed area
- Using suitable ponies to teach

The use of body protectors is very popular now. In some disciplines they are now compulsory. And in such disciplines, such as cross country, I think this is good. However, mounting and dismounting can be difficult while wearing the protector and riders may have to be helped off. They can become hooked to the saddle by the protector when dismounting. I have also known children drop to the floor as a result of getting their body protector caught up when dismounting the pony. So, for the very young children, do take extra care when they are dismounting from their pony.

Choice of Pony

The choice of pony for teaching the child is paramount. The choice also plays an important part in the avoidance of early falls. The pony needs to be of a very reliable and kind temperament. The pony needs to be responsive to light aids but must never over react. A pony that responds to voice commands can be an added bonus. The pony needs to be trained for lots of unexpected moves in the saddle as children can lose balance and make jerky movements at times. The pony needs to be quiet enough to stop if the rider falls and not one inclined run off around the arena in shock. He needs to be placid and calm in all situations. Perfect ponies are hard to come by but near perfect ones often do a brilliant job.

I had an adorable pony called Dancer. She was fast but bombproof. She was brilliant on the lead rein and very fast off! She was a delight to handle from the ground. However she did like to bite the nearest person when having her girth tightened and she would nip the handler when a rider got on board. But this little pony taught more child beginners than I care to count. Due to her speed off the lead rein she gave many children their first real gallop in the outdoors. She galloped so fast the rider was held on board by gravity itself. She would gallop as fast as any pony ever could and would always gallop to me! She was loved by so many and yet she was not perfect. We just had to treat her with respect which ponies deserve anyway. The instructor needs to weigh up any bad behaviour against the important good behaviour. If a pony is exceptionally good on the lead rein in walk and trot but bucks badly in canter you could use the pony for his good gaits and use a different pony for training the child to canter!

Age is an important factor to consider when looking for a school pony or a child's pony. Youngsters cannot be considered for the job. The minimum age for a pony to go into a school is four years. I would not consider a pony suitable for teaching children until it is well established in its training. The pony also needs to be fully developed mentally and physically. You would need to be looking at ponies aged seven years and over. There are of course exceptions to every rule so don't turn a great pony down because it's only six and a half!

If ponies are used too early to teach novices they can soon learn evasions to get themselves out of working too hard. Once a pony is mature and more established they are less likely to look for evasions. Children and beginners inadvertently offer ponies so many options that they can choose from in order to avoid certain requests. Once ponies and horses learn they can decide for themselves then they can become very difficult.

Height of the pony is debatable and a range of 12.2hh / 14.2hh should be considered. A lot will depend on the age and size of the child or children you will be teaching. It is usually recommended that children do not start serious riding lessons until they reach the age of six. I have found this a good age as below this age very little work can be achieved. I think if you have your own pony at home then the child can begin riding as soon as you feel they are able. Although little actual riding and control of the pony will be achieved, leading a child quietly around on a pony builds confidence and begins the bonding process and hopefully a lifelong passion for riding and loving ponies.

Therefore the size of the pony will be individual preference or what you have available at home. So long as the pony is quiet and can be led quietly and calmly. The riding school pony which will be purchased for the job must be neither to big or to small but the temperament must be unflappable. Avoid a pony with extravagant paces as this would not benefit a beginner. In the riding school environment a proprietor will need to buy a pony that can be ridden by various sizes of children. Therefore such ponies should be small yet weight bearing for the bigger children.

The breed of the pony is another debatable area and needs to be considered carefully. The Welsh Mountain Pony seems ideal and can often be seen at shows in the lead rein and first ridden classes. They come in a variety of shapes and sizes and train easily. Connemara ponies are a delightful breed to work with and usually have nice temperaments. Ponies crossed with the Connemara also make ideal riding ponies. Many people assume a Shetland makes a good start for children. I feel the action of the Shetland pony can be a little choppy for the complete beginner. I have also seen so many Shetlands that can bolt within a split second. Crossbred ponies of a middleweight build are used in many schools as they are sturdy and usually placid.

The Welsh Mountain pony robust and dependable

Britain has a wide variety of Native ponies to choose from. Many of these make excellent children's ponies. The New Forest Pony is a sturdy and hardy type. They can be as small as 12.2hh and as tall as 14.2hh. They are placid, gentle and train easily towards becoming reliable children's ponies. They are also sure footed and can be safely ridden over a variety of terrain.

Exmoor and Dartmoor are also Britain's Native ponies and these too make ideal children's mounts. I have seen many of these ponies in the pony club over the years. Again they are hardy, sturdy, strong, surefooted and reliable. The Dartmoor pony is a small type and should stand no larger than 12.2hh. The Dartmoor is renowned for its gentle and kind nature.

Whichever pony or ponies you decide to use, they must be fit for the job. It is no good expecting a pony to work hard in a lesson when he has been out in the field all summer getting fat. The pony needs to be prepared for the job and brought in to work slowly and sensibly over a period of time. Fitness cannot be achieved in less than eight weeks. The pony must be started in walk and, over the eight week period, building up to lengthy trotting and short bursts of canter.

Below is a suggested fitness programme for a pony being brought back into work after a lengthy period not working. Always remember to give the pony at least one day off per week. Increase the food consumption slowly as the work increases.

- Week 1 walk pony for ten minutes a day in hand

- Week 2 lunge the pony in his tack for ten minutes a day
- Week 3 walk for twenty minutes a day with short burst of trotting on the lunge
- Week 4 lunge in walk and trot for half an hour building up to forty minutes
- Week 5 as above, introduce short bursts of canter
- Week 6 increase the trotting and canter work for up to half an hour
- Week 7 increase the canter work
- Week 8 trotting and cantering preferably week 7-8 a small rider should be on board

Teaching at home or in a commercial yard the pony should not do more than two hours in succession. If the lesson you give is demanding i.e. jumping then I would give the pony a long break in between if he is to perform another lesson. With simple basic lessons in a school situation a fit pony should be capable of three to four hours maximum each.

Tack and Equipment

The first saddle for a child beginner needs to be small and comfortable. For tiny children you can purchase saddles that are not much more than a sturdy pad (club saddle). They have small girths and stirrups and more importantly a strap across the front of the saddle. This strap can be held onto by the child as they have their first lessons. As the child gains confidence the strap will be there for emergencies. If you do not obtain a saddle with a small strap then an old stirrup leather can be useful. This can be placed around the pony's neck and the rider can hold it in an emergency or during loss of balance.

If you do have D rings on the front of the saddle you can make a strap out of bailer twine. It is simple to do just plait the twine to make it a little thicker and tie it to the D rings thus creating a handy little security strap for the rider. You can also purchase a balance handle from the saddler.

The saddle must fit the child's bottom well and be neither too big nor too small. The saddle should have two rings on the front (D rings) you may need the rings for the application of a daisy rein. The daisy rein is useful if you ride on a grassed area. You will find, naturally, the pony will want to do a bit of grazing during the lesson. Even the best pony in the world will try eating grass when working on it. When the pony puts his head down it can unseat little riders and they are usually unable to stop the pony doing this. The pony thinks that because the rider does not pull his head up that he is allowed to eat the grass. This then can become a very bad habit. The daisy rein is attached from the D rings to the head piece of the bridle and this stops the action altogether. You can also make a daisy rein by using bailer twine. You can thread the twine through the D rings up through the browband and down to the bit. You must make sure that the daisy rein you make yourself does not interfere with the movement of the pony to much. A homemade daisy rein is useful when you suddenly find yourself in need of one. I am giving away my secret life of being a farmer's wife! Bailer twine is used in all repairs and modifications around the farm and livestock.

A D ring on the back of the saddle will also prove helpful if the saddle slips forward. I often find that ponies can have this problem no matter how well the saddle fits. Especially in the summer when the ponies can become rather round! A crupper will cure the problem, it is a leather strap that goes under the pony's tail and attaches to the D ring on the back of the saddle. Always allow the pony to become accustomed to the feel of the crupper without the rider. Some may buck when they first feel it in the dock region.

A home made crupper works really well and is much more cost effective! Baler twine (you guessed it) is plaited, making sure you leave a large loop at one end (for under the tail) and enough twine to attach to the D rings at the back of the saddle. Make sure that the twine that goes under the tail is covered for comfort. I used a travel tail guard as it gave a good padding for the area. If you do not have a D ring on the back of the saddle you can purchase a little attachment at the saddle shop. It is an attachable D ring that just slips into the gullet and secures itself. It can be added or removed at any time which is rather handy.

Most importantly of all the saddle must fit the pony. It must give a good clearance to the withers and spine. It must sit stable upon the ponies back while working. There must be no sign of rubbing or discomfort when the saddle is removed after work. I am a great believer in the amazing gel pads as opposed to numnahs when considering placing the saddle on the pony. Numnahs are ok but I feel that they are more liable to rub and cause discomfort. The gel pad spreads all weight of the saddle and rider evenly throughout the ponies back thus preventing any pressure points. Ponies can often become difficult when they are in discomfort. It would be possible for their behaviour to become unpredictable and even dangerous in their attempt to get away from whatever is causing pain. This could even result in bucking etc.

The stirrup irons must be of the safety variety. Peacock safety stirrups must not be used as these can actually be very dangerous. When dismounting I have known them to not only rip jodhpurs but also a child's flesh! It is therefore vital that these are not used. The swan neck variety has always worked very well with the children I have taught. I have found them to be very safe and reliable for children and adults. The irons must not be too big as the child's foot might travel all the way through the iron thus trapping the foot in the iron. Nor do you want the child's foot squeezed into a small iron as this too would cause the foot to become trapped. The iron should clear the child's foot by at least an adult finger width each side. When checking the length of the stirrups allow the child's leg to hang next to the iron on the end of the leather. The bottom of the iron should just touch the child's ankle. Stand at the front of the pony and check that both the stirrups are the same length on each side. The child will ride better when correctly balanced, more importantly a level rider will reduce undue stress on the pony's back.

Leathers must be junior size as adult sizes will require twists in them to accommodate smaller legs. Twists are not really safe as they can make the stirrups rigid and unyielding should the child part company with the pony. This will render even safety stirrups not as reliable as they should be. Twists in the leathers will also alter the angle of the rider's foot and lower leg. This in turn can reduce the required flexibility of the ankle area. Your local saddle shop should be able to sell you a set of hole punchers enabling you to alter the size of the leather safely and correctly.

A pony suitable for children should be snaffle mouth in the first instance. I find that a thick rubber bit is ideal as this is very soft on the corners of the mouth. Although I try hard to insist no balance is obtained by the rider via the reins, unfortunately it is sometimes inevitable. Therefore, choose the gentlest snaffle you can obtain.

A mounting block is important as it is now evident that mounting from the ground is detrimental to the health of the ponies back. You should make sure that you purchase or make a sturdy and safe mounting block that cannot be unbalanced with a child on board. Remember though, it is still important that a child is taught to mount from the ground for emergency mounting. Also, later on, when hacking out, the rider may need to dismount to open gates etc.

Clothing for the Rider

A hard hat up to current standards must be worn at all times on and around the ponies. The hat must fit well and it is advisable to have a child's hat professionally fitted. Never purchase a second hand hat as you do not know if it has been banged during falls. Once a hat has been involved in a bad fall it must be disposed of. During a bad fall when the helmet is involved i.e. head injury, the hat can suffer minor weakening that would render it less effective during any future impact.

A young rider well turned out but the hood must be removed before riding

Gloves should be worn to avoid chaffing of the delicate fingers and to keep the hands warm in cold weather. Gloves will also help prevent the reins slipping through the Childs fingers. Footwear must be sturdy with a small heel to prevent the foot slipping through the stirrup iron. I often advise Wellington boots in the first instance, although this would only be for the first few lessons to see if the child takes to riding. Most children have a pair of wellingtons and riding boots can be an expensive outlay in the beginning, if the child does not take to riding then money is wasted. Wellington boots are long, giving protection from stirrup leathers pinching the lower leg. Wellingtons also have a suitable size heel and support for the ankle. A sensible coat should be worn making sure that it does not have a hood attached unless of course you can fold it away. No toggles or flapping bits should be present. It is surprising how an innocent coat can cause injuries when riding ponies. The coat must always be fastened when the child is on or around ponies.

In hot weather do not allow the child to ride in a short sleeved top. You must always make sure that the child's arms are covered in case of a fall. It is surprising that a long sleeve can reduce grazes etc. In hot sunny weather it is also wise to remind parents to apply sun cream to their children! Also fly repellent when necessary.

If you are teaching little girls it is preferable to ask them to tie hair back in a low pony tail. The fine hair of little girls can blow all over their face making riding difficult. Remove any hair clips as these can cause injury in a fall. Also hair clips will cause pressure points under the hat and this will hurt the child. Plaits are fine so long as they are below the hat. Braided hair under the riding hat can cause pressure points that will become sore and even cause headaches.

It is very important to notice if any child is chewing gum. This can be missed if you are teaching a group as some children even keep it stored in their mouth. Chewing gum can kill a child if it suddenly ends up in the windpipe. As ponies are unpredictable at times this could happen if one jogged of suddenly or tripped etc. Make sure all chewing gum, or anything else they are eating, is removed before they mount the pony. Also do not allow children to ride with earrings etc as this can prove dangerous round ponies.

In these modern times it is crucial to mention the dreaded mobile phone. Often children think it is acceptable to take calls when on a lesson. However, always make sure phones are at least switched off or silent. The different ring tones can upset a pony unexpectedly, especially heavy metal and I say this after witnessing a terrible incident involving such a ring tone on horseback.

Facilities required

An enclosure is ideal but not always available. If you have an enclosure or ménage then that is great. If you have not then you will just need to keep the child on the lead rein longer than normal. Children can also do a lot of practice riding down quiet lanes etc. Of course they must always be on the lead rein and both rider and leader must wear bright high visibility clothing.

A good leader is very important when training children. The leader has to be experienced and reliable. They must be aware of the rider at all times and never let their thoughts wonder. They must be old enough to concentrate and be able to control the pace and direction of the pony during early lessons. They need to be fairly fit in order to be able to run with the pony during the trot, canter and over small fences. The leader should also be wearing the correct clothing for safety and practical purposes. A hard hat must be worn along with gloves. A sturdy pair of boots should be worn to support the ankles and protect the heels while the leader is running. The boots will protect the leader from any accidental strikes from the hooves. The lead rope should be attached to the noseband of the pony to avoid any discomfort in the mouth area. You can also purchase, or even make, a bit coupling that will allow you to place the coupling on both bit rings and attach the lead rope to the middle.

If you are training children in a riding school then the ratio of pupils to instructor should be no more than six. Once above this number you will find it difficult to keep all riders within view. An instructor needs to be aware of all small riders as they can often get into unexpected difficulties. They can get distressed, tearful and even unbalanced; the instructor needs to be aware of such situations as soon as is humanly possible.

Duration of Lessons

In my experience with children's lessons a good length of lesson is a maximum of thirty minutes. I feel that for young children any longer can prove too tiring. They lose concentration and become tired and irritable. Not only do children become tired mentally but also physically. They only have little limbs and the work required to ride is very demanding on both counts. If a child begins riding at six/seven years old I have found half an hour perfectly adequate up to the age of ten. If the child wants to ride more then they would benefit from having lessons twice weekly for the half hour duration. This would be more beneficial than having an hour lesson once a week.

Where to Ride

You can obtain a list of licensed riding schools from your local authority. I would consider word of mouth to be important in finding the right school. If people already ride there and recommend it, then that is a good start. Be wary of any instructor or school that does not like parents to watch. I feel that it is important for the parents to have the option to be present as their young children learn to ride. Particularly during early lessons when the child is at their most vulnerable. As you get to know the instructor and you feel happy with them teaching your child you can gradually wean yourself away and encourage independence from your child. Riding is a high risk sport so it is important that you observe an instructor teaching your child to make sure you are happy with their attitude and competence. If the instructor does not make you feel welcome to watch the lesson I would be tempted to find an instructor who does.

If you are not relaxed and happy with the instructor then you must not leave your child with them. Change the instructor or school until you are happy with the person in charge of your child. Not everyone has the ability to teach children. It requires a lot of patience and a genuine fondness for kids. If the instructor does not have a genuine fondness for children the child will feel this and fail to blossom well as a rider.

Riding for children is all about having fun in a safe friendly environment. A teacher tolerating children on a pony will not be able to give them that sense of fun that is so vital.

Remember that the child rider is just starting out. The instructor you choose is laying down the foundations for the future riding of your child. It is a chance as an instructor to mould the child to be a competent and confident rider. I feel strongly that as an instructor you are also developing the child's attitude towards ponies and animals in general. On a personal note, if the instructor encourages punishment for the ponies as opposed to rewarding them for good work then I would be wary. Many schools encourage children early on to use the whip without any thought to the feelings of the animals. Often riders are taught to over use the whip as opposed to being taught to ride correctly. I always try to discourage use of the whip so that it does not become accepted by the child as normal. After all they would not take a whip to the family dog!

Qualities of a Children's Instructor

Some may disagree when I say that to teach children you have to like them. I don't believe you can give the child what they want/need without a genuine affinity with them. The instructor must teach every client throughout the day as if they were the first client of the day. This requires enthusiasm and enjoyment in what they are doing. You must remember that although a group of children may be your fifth lesson of the day this is their first and only lesson of the day!

Not every instructor will like to teach children and to do so is a vocation. You must find an instructor who does like to teach children and young people. The instructor should be cheerful and passionate about their work. They need to be well turned out and punctual for their clients. They must have the required patience to deal with children on ponies. They must instil confidence in the children they are teaching. The instructor must display nothing but patience in all situations met during the lessons.

The instructor must take all events in their stride. They must remain calm and in control during all events and situations. No matter how they feel inside they must portray to the pupils that everything is just fine! Make light of all situations that occur during the riding lesson. Of course this does not include situations that are of a nature brought about by disobedience of the child rider. Nor does it include behaviour from the child that causes the pony to suffer discomfort. Such incidents must be treated seriously.

The instructor must have an in depth knowledge of their subject. Qualifications for the job of riding teacher are helpful and indicate that the teacher has put in the theory and practical. However don't discount an instructor without formal qualifications. Some instructors have a lot of experience without such certificates. Some have been very busy out there doing various disciplines. Such instructors that have competed over a period of time will not have had the chance to gain qualifications. Similarly you may find an instructor that has been teaching for many years, not managing to find the time or the money to get the qualifications in place.

Motivation is a very important quality of the instructor. Without being motivated themselves, it would be more difficult to motivate the riders. There is little worse than being taught by an instructor who does not actually want to be teaching, it does happen.

An instructor must be able to communicate well with all their pupils young or old. Not only is verbal communication necessary but also the ability to communicate in a non verbal way. They should be able to read the unspoken language of a child in the saddle. Children will tell you so much just by facial expressions and body language. If they will not admit they are afraid to do something verbally it will often manifest physically. There are of course signs to look for if a child tries to fool you in to thinking they are happy to do the work you ask of them;

- Tense muscles all over the body
- Rigid posture
- Holding their breath for long periods
- Abnormally pale Face
- Dry mouth
- Folding into a near foetal position
- Tears
- Irritability and snappiness
- Extreme laughter (yes it can happen)
- Frowning

I always stress to children that they do not have to perform any command that they are not happy with. Many young children feel that they have to do everything an adult tells them, especially the very young. Often they do not want to and yet they can't express this reluctance. I feel it is important that they know they can express this at any moment they are not happy. I emphasise it as I feel it will hopefully carry over to other areas in their young lives when they feel a need to say no.

Rather often I have come across children who carry baggage with them to their riding lessons. By this, I mean that, whatever negativity goes on in their everyday life, particularly school, or even home, can affect how they ride. We have all seen what confidence can do. It can make you ride well and positively. However, often, when children turn up for a riding lesson, any negative experience that they have encountered during the week can have serious detrimental effect. It can leave them lacking confidence and feeling rather inadequate.

I have noticed over the years that out of the blue pupils riding ability can go down hill rapidly when unsettled by outside forces. You may find yourself in the situation of having to try and delve a little to get to the route of the problem. All sorts of problems can come to the surface but I find that commonly a child may be suffering from being bullied by peers. This can severely affect the children's confidence in the saddle. To simply be aware of such situations can help you to adapt your lessons accordingly. And it also helps you to understand why the child may not be learning so well that day.

Problems a child may encounter that will affect confidence and ability on the pony

- Bullying from peers
- Family problems
- Family break up
- A death in the family
- Health problems
- Someone they love may be ill
- Worry about a pet

Many children are found to be having problems at school and at home. Whatever the problem may be it often seems to be huge and all consuming to a small child.

Allow the child to tell you as much as they want to get off their chest. Listen with a sympathetic ear while encouraging the child to continue riding. Obviously with a group lesson you would have to make sure that you did not neglect your other pupils. Although with regular groups you will find that each individual will need extra care and attention at some stage during their time with you!

Praise must always be given to children when they are trying their best. As you praise a child the pleasure they get from it is instant. You can almost see them grow an inch in stature as a result. Praise can never really be overdone. Criticism is also important but must be carried out constructively.

Example

My pupil may be asking for a canter and fail to get it. I will say something like, "well tried, that was a good effort and, although you did not get the canter, the trot became lovely as a result of what you were doing, well done." After discussing ways to improve the transition we will then attempt the transition again. No matter how bad a child or an adult rides there is always something positive to speak about along with any negative. Remember your last words spoken as the lesson ends must be positive!

At the end of each lesson finish with a simple exercise that the child knows well and can perform well. It is no good starting on complicated work in the last 15 minutes as it could all go horribly wrong. This would end the lesson negatively.

Even if the lesson finishes a little early with a grand finish this will leave the child feeling good about their riding. Also the pony will feel rewarded for his good efforts.

What to do in the event of a fall

It is important to be aware of falling riders. Though we always hope there are no falls, you must be able to deal with them when they occur. It would be ideal if children never fell off, but sadly, accidents do happen. No instructor is super human and cannot control all situations involving the ponies. We must do our best to prevent falls, while also being aware that the ponies can never be predictable all of the time. They will always have instincts that can often override sensible behaviour.

If and when a child falls off, the instructor must keep calm and be reassuring to the child. Make sure that they remain in the position they landed until you get to them. Any movement of the fallen rider must be slow, do not allow the rider to jump to their feet. This seems to be a shock reaction and they can often collapse down again. Once a fall is in progress I tend to watch closely as the rider lands. You can usually asses the severity of the fall at this stage.

I keep a very close eye as the rider hits the ground, I am looking primarily that the head does not take a great impact. If it does then at least I am aware. It is wise to see which part of the body hits the ground first as sometimes riders are unaware and confused.

If the rider is unconscious or cannot feel their legs an ambulance must be called immediately. If the rider is just shocked and winded talk to them in a calm manner and make light of the situation. When a child falls from the pony the resulting screaming can be rather scary for all concerned. It is usually from shock, not pain, and they will need reassuring that they are alright and it is over. I have noticed with very young children they often become hysterical in a way that suggests they are afraid that the incident is still ongoing. Almost like they are expecting even worse to come, though we know the accident has run its course.

With a conscious rider, distressed or not, it is still vital to carefully asses the situation. You do not want to be placing a rider back in the saddle that could possibly have an injury undetected by you and the rider themselves. Usually a gentle manipulation of the various body parts will identify any minor bruising or possible sprains/ breaks. If you have observed the fall closely you should be more aware of the injured areas. Slowly and gently help the rider to their feet and make sure they are happy and well enough to remount.

Try to get the rider on board again for at least a walk round the arena. Finish the lesson on a good note and praise the rider for bravery. On rare occasions you may not be able to get the rider back into the saddle for various reasons. They may be too shocked or shaken up. They may be in too much pain. You will have to respect the rider's decision not to remount as it is unwise to force the issue. You will simply have to deal with the situation when the next lesson comes round. The memory of the incident may mean that the rider will benefit from riding a different pony.

Make sure that the parents are aware of the fall and fill them in on as much detail as possible. Remember to write up the incident in your accident book!
You must record;

- The name of the pony
- The date and time of the fall
- The details of how it happened
- What caused it
- The injuries sustained
- The procedure you followed
- Follow up

If a particular pony is entered into the accident book on numerous occasions you must decide whether he is suitable for the job.

Be aware that the rider will probably carry the fear with them for the next few lessons. Go back a few stages and progress slowly to rebuild confidence.

First Aid Kit

The first aid kit should always be easily accessible for the instructor or assistant. It is important to keep up your first aid knowledge. There are many courses available at colleges or similar. The British horse Society requires that you hold a first aid certificate in order to be added to their instructors list.

The most important item of my kit, I have found over the years, is an ice pack. You can buy ice packs these days that just sit dormant until you need them. When they are required you simply have to put pressure on a little hard spot in the ice pack. This then activates the package and it becomes cold very quickly. It is then applied to the injured area. The ice pack is ideal for impact injuries such as a kick. If applied immediately they can reduce swelling and bruising very effectively. Failing to have an ice pack to hand a bag of frozen peas works well! If using a package from the freezer, make sure that you do not put it directly on the skin. This could cause a freezer burn. Wrap the item in a piece of cloth before placing it against the skin.

Other important items include:

- Eye wash
- Antiseptic ointment and wipes
- Plasters
- Sling/bandages
- Scissors
- Lint

Always remember it is only minor injuries that you will deal with. Anything major such as loss of consciousness breaks or large open injuries must be treated as an emergency. Call an ambulance immediately!

Chapter 2

Introduction to riding

The first lessons must be considered as the foundations for the future of the rider. These first lessons should not only instil confidence of the rider; more importantly the attitude of the child rider towards their pony will also be engrained at this stage. All too often children are taught to kick hard to go and pull hard to stop. That is roughly about it! It is imperative at this stage that the rider is taught to treat the pony with the utmost respect and to stroke or pat the pony when he has performed well.

The rider must be taught to give signals to the pony in the lightest of manners. If we ask with a whisper (gently in our manner) and we are ignored we can then start to increase the signals and the strength. If we start with a screaming signal then where we do go from there? Many ponies that appear to be stubborn when riders are kicking hard at their sides will simply require a more gentle approach.

Problems should not be encountered at this stage as the pony you have chosen for the lessons should know his job. They will be on the lead rein anyway, thus reducing the opportunity for bad behaviour. However the child should be encouraged to carry a whip at a later stage. They must be educated in the use of the whip as an aid to good riding. The whip should not be used as a punishment nor should it take the place of good legs for getting forwardness.

Many times I have witnessed riders giving poor signals to their pony. They have then been taught that, if the pony does not respond to poor signals, then the whip needs to be applied. I consider the teaching of child riders a great opportunity to educate them that the pony is not a machine and ponies are sentient beings that do feel pain. The young riders should carry this vital teaching with them throughout their career. They also need to be made aware that whipping a pony or horse is unacceptable. If, in the future, they are ever told to whip their pony they must be aware they do not have to do anything they are uncomfortable with. To respect the pony will be taught over the months ahead and must always be reaffirmed at every opportunity.

The first lesson

The first few lessons for the child will have a huge impact as to whether they take to life in the saddle or not. Although riding is an unpredictable sporting activity it is up to you as an instructor to do everything humanly possible to prevent falls at this delicate stage. You will have the chosen pony waiting complete with tack to introduce to the new rider. Make sure they have a little time patting and getting to know the pony. The pony must be on the lead rein and have a suitable neck or saddle strap for several lessons at least.

Keep the language around a child rider simple. Children don't want to have to deal with big complicated words and explanations. It is simple for the child if you use language that is part of their everyday vocabulary. For example the near side and off side of the pony is of little relevance to the child. However left and right side of the pony will make it a little easier. Do bear in mind that young children may even struggle with left and right. Use this opportunity to introduce them to the concept. You could even encourage them to write a big R and a big L on each glove! Possibly parents could sew the letters onto the child's gloves.

Asking the child to take the outside leg back behind the girth for a canter transition would be difficult as they have to work hard just staying on board. There will be plenty of time in the future to go back to the beginning and refine the aids etc. The very basics need to be taught at this stage.

- Show the child how to mount with a demonstration from one of your helpers if possible.

- Demonstrate how to hold the reins correctly

- Position the child correctly in the saddle

- Explain how to make the pony walk by squeezing with the legs (a very small child may need the instructor or a helper giving a little bit of physical support during movement)

- How to make the pony stop by pulling gently on the reins

- Practice walking and halting as this will give the child confidence in his ability to stop the pony which will make him feel in control of the situation

- Show the child how to dismount (during early dismounting you may need to give the child a little support during landing on the ground)

You should find that the above brings you to the end of the lesson and that is just enough for the first session.

Lesson 2

This will be a repeat of lesson one; however, we can now introduce steering the pony. Steering can be introduced here and this can be practiced in and out of cones. If you don't have cones then any large objects that pony and rider can weave in and out of will be suitable. Always make sure that the child is taught to turn by taking the rein away from the neck to direct the turn. Many riders naturally pull back to turn the pony this must be discouraged to avoid losing forwardness. You could include some simple rein changes remembering to explain why we work the pony equally on both reins. It is vital in order to develop muscles evenly and to make the pony supple on both sides.

Lesson 3

Lesson three will be a repeat of lesson one and two. Five minutes before the end of the second lesson the trot can be introduced. You must explain to the rider that the trot can be rather bouncy. It is important that you warn them as it can be a little surprising for the rider. Before the child has experienced their first trot I do not usually discuss the actual mechanics. I like them to feel the trot and then talk about what they have felt and why the trot feels the way it does. Make sure that the trot is introduced very slowly. The leader must be instructed to do no more than two or three strides to start with. If the child is happy then you can slowly increase the number of trot strides. Finish the lesson on a good note with a bit of a trot. Leave the child looking forward to the next lesson and eager to trot some more!

At this stage it is useful to introduce the child to leading their pony out of the arena. Children seem to get really excited about this and it gives them great pleasure to feel they are involved with care of the pony. Make sure they take the reins over the head and show them how to run up the stirrups. Repetition is vital; it can take many times to learn to run up the stirrups. Point out to the child why we do certain things, such as running up stirrups, as it is important they know that it is for safety. Over the coming weeks try and introduce the child to the safety rules around ponies.

Safety around the Pony

- Never walk behind the pony always walk round the front to avoid being kicked
- Never move hastily round the pony as you may frighten him or make him jump
- Always be calm and quiet while talking gently to the pony
- Explain about the vision of ponies and the blind spots (blind directly infront of the head due to eyes being on the side of his head, and blind directly behind the bum

- Teach them how and why we loosen the girth when we have finished riding. Make sure they are aware of things we do to make the pony comfortable.

Lesson 4

Repeat previous lessons, building on the trot work. The rising trot must be demonstrated and practiced. Most children perform the rising trot well, although often lacking style.

Children grasp the rising trot well if you guide them through it at standstill. I always use the term forward and back as opposed to up and down when describing the rising trot. Children work every part of their body if you say up and down. They appear to be climbing a steep mountain with even the arms flapping in an upward motion. Sometimes the motion is such as they look ready to ping out of the saddle. I find forward and back works better and keeps them steady in the saddle. Sometimes you may need to help them physically with your hand at the base of their spine urging them forward.

I consider the rising trot to be one of the hardest lessons the pupil will have to learn. It requires patience from the instructor. Riders will develop at different speeds and timescales. A good instructor will simply encourage without rushing the child.

You will find that the child will manage just one rise every few strides. This one rise must be praised readily and the child encouraged. As they continue to practice you will notice that one rise every few strides becomes two rises every few strides and so on. Patience is required and will be rewarded soon enough.

It seems to work better if you tell the child when to rise in the saddle. I normally say "up" and let them come down themselves as this is unavoidable. Therefore they can respond better listening to one command. I always insist they land in the saddle with the utmost care as soon as they are able. They find it amusing when I ask them to imagine half a dozen eggs under their bum on landing!

Lesson 5

This lesson will also be a repeat of the previous lessons. Add a little more trotting at the end of the lesson. Exercises can be introduced to give the child a bit of extra stimulation. Exercises such as round the world will be considered as great fun by children. Such exercises can also build confidence and balance.

Suggested Exercises

- Round the World
- Half scissors
- Full Scissors
- Thread the Needle
- Balancing in the saddle while standing up in the stirrups

Round the world consist of the rider simply lifting their leg over the front of the pony. The rider will then be sat side saddle. The rider then takes their leg over again, this will leave them sitting facing the rear of the pony. One more lifting of the leg will leave the rider side saddle again. The leg is lifted over the front of the pony and the rider will be back to the beginning. Little riders will need a lot of support as, initially, it is easy to lose balance.

Half scissors involves the rider taking their leg over the front to sit side saddle again. Then they will flip onto their belly and raise the opposite leg over the front of the pony. This will again leave them facing the rear of the pony. Performed a second time will take them back to the correct position in the saddle.

Full scissors is more complicated and harder to achieve. The rider swings both legs backwards so that he is laid, tummy down, flat on the back of the pony. The rider will then flip over onto his back and sit up facing the back of the pony. Repeat to take the rider back to the correct position.

Thread the needle is a simple and fun exercise. The rider leaves one foot in the stirrup i.e. left leg and brings the opposite leg, right leg, over the front of the saddle. The rider will then thread the free leg, right leg, under the leg that is still in the stirrup, left leg. This is where the threading the needle comes in. Once the right leg has thread through the left leg the rider will then take the right leg over the back as if remounting the pony.

Standing in the stirrups speaks for itself. Simple but effective this exercise is so good for strength of core muscles. Also confidence builds, especially if the child manages to walk around the arena.

Subsequent Lessons

Over the coming weeks the lessons will be a repeat of all the above. Using your imagination will help to avoid monotony. The canter should not be introduced until the rising trot is established and the child is happy and confident in their riding. A good instructor will be aware that no two children are the same. They learn at different paces, some are slower than others. Patience must be used at all times with any kind of teaching. Never rush a pupil into any advancement until they are truly ready. To do this is risky and can undo all the good work already in place.

As an instructor it is sensible not to rush any child. Lay down firm foundations which will help to build rider confidence. Patience will pay dividends in the fact you will have taught your pupils thoroughly and well.

When to come off the Lead Rein

With a true schoolmaster pony the child can be taken off the lead rein as soon as their balance is established at the walk and trot. You must use your experience and intuition in making this decision. If you do not feel experienced enough then seek advice of someone who is. Some of you reading this book may be teaching children for the first time or even teaching because the rider is your own child. In such cases you will not have the necessary experience required to make such decisions. You cannot afford to get it wrong so do ask someone who knows.

If the pony you are using is anything less than perfect (some of you will not have a vast choice at your finger tips) then the child must be kept on the lead rein for as long as is necessary. It is always better with the child rider to proceed with caution and leave them on the lead rein longer. This would be more beneficial than taking them off too soon!

Lunge Lessons

Although not always practical I do feel it is important to talk a little bit about lunge lessons. Lunge lessons are obviously private as you can only do one at a time. They are also short lessons as they are very intense. I feel 15/20 minutes is ample for pony and rider

Often when teaching you will find that riders can hang onto bad habits. An example is a little girl who I taught that spent all her early lessons in a forward position due to fear. She felt that sitting in a forward position was safer. I think it put her nearer to the ponies' neck and that made her feel secure. There was no way on earth we could cure the problem during a class lesson. I therefore put her on the lunge for three lessons and was able to correct the positional fault during this time.

The above is just an example; you will come across many faults that require a couple of lunge lessons to sort out. Lunge lessons can be more expensive so may not be practical for some pupils. You can work on so much with a rider on the lunge. It is helpful how the rider relaxes knowing that you are controlling the pony. They feel safe and secure and can therefore concentrate on what you are asking of them.

The pony used for a lunge lesson must, of course, have experience working on the lunge line. They must listen to the instructor during each of the paces. Some ponies can find the lunge line a little exciting in which case you should lunge them without the rider first in order to allow initial excitement to be dispersed.

The pony should be wearing brushing boots all round to avoid any injury to his legs. The rider's safety, as usual, is paramount as in all their riding activities. Removal of the stirrups is acceptable but a neck strap or saddle strap must be in place. It is also acceptable to take away the reins and tie them in a knot. However it is unwise to remove both the stirrups and reins at the same time.

If you are going to work the rider without stirrups they must have well established balance. Make sure that the circle you lunge on is large as this will help the rider to stay in balance. Removal of the reins is a good exercise if you have a rider that relies on them for balance. It will surprise the rider how well they will manage without them. This will help them to accept that they do not need the reins to stay on the pony.

Work without stirrups will help with balance and confidence. A deeper seat will be encouraged. The rider will hopefully ride with longer stirrups as a result of the deeper seat developed with this type of work.

Lunging is tiring for both pony and rider so do use it in moderation. When a pony is lunged you will notice that the inside limbs and joints do take a lot of strain. Always be sure the pony is fit and sound for use on the lunge. Any pony that has a history of joint problems or any form of unsoundness in the limbs or back must never be subjected to lunge lessons. Ponies with any form of limb or back problems can still be used for teaching in the school (with veterinary guidance) but never on the lunge!

Things to consider when lunging the pony

- Always perform the work equally on both reins (both directions) so all muscles and joints are loaded the same.

- Always use only sound ponies for this strenuous work

- 20 minutes is ample for a lunge lesson (half hour max)

- Always put protective boots on the pony

- Only use a fit pony for a lunge lesson

- Warm up the pony well before lunging with a rider

Chapter 3 Advancing the Rider

The half halt

There are many instructors that would not introduce the half halt so early on in the rider's career. However, I like to teach the half halt early on as it helps the pony to remain comfortable and can reduce the riders need to pull. Even if the child is not ever so good at the half halt, introducing it early on will allow the child to develop it over the coming months. The basics of early riding consist of kick to go and pull to stop. This is riding at its most raw. It is important that we refine the rider at the earliest opportunity. Refinement of the rider will make life much more comfortable for the pony. The half halt, even when ridden other than perfect, can serve very useful. I encourage the children to use the half halt to slow the pony down, rather than pulling strongly on the pony's mouth. The results have been amazing and it is surprising how well the child responds to learning the half halt. It is just that, we are asking the pony to halt but only for a second and then we ride them on. As I watch the results before me I realise that it must make the working life of the pony much better.

When the child pulls on the reins to slow a pony down the pony pulls harder and can certainly often out pull the child. Yet if they use the half halt the pony seems to respond much quicker and the pulling battle between pony and rider is almost eliminated.

In a split second the rider must perform the following:

- Sit tall
- Squeeze with the legs

- Take and give the outside rein (some will understand the term squeeze and release)

It must be made clear that the half halt should be ridden for a second only. The rider can do it many times if need be but it must only ever last a second!

It is vital that it is instilled in the rider that the half halt is *take and give.* Many riders misunderstand and *give then take.* To give then take with the reins serves no purpose except to cause discomfort to the pony.

The Half halt will be used in so many situations:

- To maintain a pace
- To maintain rhythm and tempo
- To prepare for a movement or change of pace
- To alert the pony that he is about to receive a command
- To rebalance
- Most of all to reduce the need for pulling on the pony's mouth

The Sitting Trot

Before we introduce the canter it is important to teach the child how to sit to the trot. The child will need to be able to sit to the trot in order to ask the pony to canter. I don't like to spend too much time working on the sitting trot as I consider it rather detrimental to a pony that is used for many children's lessons. The sitting trot can be rather taxing for the pony and the rider. Always make sure that the pony is well worked in before you even think about performing the sitting trot. The large muscle along the back will struggle to take the continual impact of the rider if he has not been worked in and the muscles warmed up sufficiently. An older pony will cope better with the demands of the sitting trot.

When the sitting trot is ridden well the rider will absorb the concussion arising from the movement. However, when a novice is being taught sitting trot, the pony's back will take the brunt of the concussion. Too much of this type of work will be tiring and could cause the pony to hollow his back. A hollow back is a weaker back and injuries from weakening the back could occur.

Introduce the sitting trot a little at a time as done with the rising trot. At first the feeling to the rider will be unsettling and there will be a loss of balance, the rider will become stiff and tense. You need to try and encourage the rider to stay relaxed and soft throughout their body. This will be easier said than done. Just ask the rider to cease rising in the trot for two strides only. Gradually increase the number of sitting strides until they are completing the short side of the school. This will be plenty of sitting trot to enable a good canter transition. I cannot emphasise enough that the sitting trot must be worked on minimally using a school pony, or any hard working pony come to that. Until the sitting trot is performed really well it is a big strain on the pony's back.

The best trot to help a rider learn the sitting trot is a slow trot. A slower trot will keep the pony round through the back and this will help the rider to sit better and reduce the bouncing. A fast trot will probably unbalance the child rather rapidly.

The Canter

Once the sitting trot is established (this could be some time) the canter, though unsettling at the start, is a wonderful pace to teach. The rider must be warned that the canter is bouncy and may feel scary to start with. I will explain to the child that we will start the canter with just two/three strides of the pace. I always find that the first couple of attempts bring various reactions from the child. They normally are rather shocked by the feel of it which is why it is so vital to slow the pony to a trot after a couple of strides. The rider can also lose balance in a drastic manner. The mere act of slowing the pony to a trot quickly and quietly will ensure the little rider feels safe in the knowledge that they are under control.

You need a very confident and established leader that will demonstrate to the child in their care that they are in total control of the pony. Only canter on straight lines as this will aid with balance.

The pony used to teach the canter must be reliable and well on the aids (responsive to requests from the rider). It is ideal if the pony can respond to the voice of the instructor and eventually the rider also. If the pony takes to long to go into canter this can be difficult and the child may be out of balance before the canter begins.

As with all areas of teaching children to ride, do keep it simple. It is no good asking them to take the outside leg back etc. I will always simply instruct them to sit to the trot and increase lower leg pressure (kick a little harder, can be a simpler command for the very young). When instructing the child to sit to the trot, it is better that they sit just as they ask for the canter. If they sit too early before they want the transition their seat can become less balanced and less deep. This will reduce the chance of a good canter transition. I also suggest that they feel a little excited. It is amazing how a little feel of excitement can build impulsion. I will often encourage children to think of Christmas morning!

Make sure the children are holding the front of the saddle or the neck strap. The initial loss of balance caused by the canter, particularly the transition, will soon subside. This must be explained to the child before you start. I would normally introduce canter towards the end of the lesson as we did with the trot. Try and make it a very positive experience so they come back wanting more.

Explain to the child how to get the canter (keep it simple):

- Get a good forward, working trot (lots of impulsion)
- Hold the front of the saddle or neck strap
- Sit deep in the saddle/stop rising
- Kick a little harder than normal
- Ask on the corner

Once the child is over the initial shock that the canter first produces you can start to increase the length of the canter. Do not complicate the lessons with refining the canter. There is plenty of time for refinement of aids, position etc once the pace and balance is established. So long as the child is encouraged to sit correctly at all times, even during mid lesson discussions. I often find that when riders (young or old) are bought in to the middle of the arena for a discussion they suddenly thrust their legs forward and slump as if in an armchair. Riders must have it instilled from an early age that once they are in the saddle they must sit correctly until they dismount. The pony is not an armchair and finds it more difficult to carry (even at standstill) a slumped rider.

Once the child becomes accustomed to the movement of the canter they usually begin to enjoy the sensation. The transition needs to be worked on during the lesson. It can be tiring for a pony to be cantering around the arena too many times during a lesson. You need to consider that it is the transition that is difficult to do well. It is the transition that will actually need the work so keep the canter short.

Although when advancing in the child's riding we will need to avoid the pony anticipating commands, sometimes we can use this anticipation to our advantage in the early stages. So if the pony is used to cantering in a certain place then we should perhaps encourage this for training purposes.

The Rein Back

Again I like to teach rein back early on in a child's career. This is simply because it is easy for the child to learn and is helpful towards developing the riders feel on the reins. I have noticed also that child riders get a real buzz out of making their pony go backwards. The rein back will also prove useful as the child progresses. It is so important to teach any riding properly but the rein back seems to always be taught so badly. I have noticed this over many years of judging the riding classes at shows. Every single rider I see attempt the rein back, performs it in the most horrible manner. Tugging and pulling on the reins is not only uncomfortable for the pony but is bad manners and looks unsightly.

The pony should already be capable of reining back when asked correctly. First the pony should be ridden to a halt. Explain the aids clearly to the child as with any new exercise.

- Sit up tall
- Take a good feel on the reins
- Ask the pony to walk forward
- Hold the reins just enough to make sure the pony cannot walk forward
- Continue asking the pony to walk while not allowing him to go forward (this should encourage the pony to go backwards)
- Keep both legs in exactly the same position at the girth

The pony should simply walk backwards as he is unable to walk forwards. Once taught properly it is a pleasure to watch. Remember taught badly it is unsightly at the very least and at the most it is pointless and detrimental to the pony.

When performed correctly the pony will do the rein back by moving his legs in diagonal pairs. This makes the foot falls the same as in trot.

Trotting Poles

Trotting poles are a vital part of a riders training. The rider and pony benefit in the following areas:

- Pony and rider balance
- Pony and rider co-ordination

- Pony will become more supple
- Pony and rider introduction to jumping (Pony used must obviously already be established in this work)
- Variety
- Obedience
- Encourages joint mobility of the pony
- Helps to increase or decrease the pony's stride length
- Helps slow a pony down if rushing into fences

Children love to do trotting poles and you must make sure the children are trained to do them correctly. As with any of your lessons ensure that the foundations are correctly laid down as the poles will eventually become jumps!

Trotting poles must be placed at a distance of around 4ft/4ft6inches apart for ponies. You should always use an odd number of poles as this will prevent a pony attempting to jump them. Watch as the pony trots over the poles as the hind feet should land in the centre. This indicates that the poles are at an ideal spacing. Most ponies can do three poles really well but may need the strides shortening beyond three, e.g. five poles means you may have to start at 4ft six and after the third shorten slightly to encourage the pony if he tires.

Explain to the children reasons why we do trotting poles. It is wise also to explain that ponies prefer not to have to flex the lower limbs, hocks etc. Therefore the rider will need to use a stronger leg at the poles to encourage flexion of the joints.

You don't have to use trotting poles just for trotting over. They are a very versatile piece of equipment. They can be used for various exercises and even games;

- Place two trotting poles side by side about four feet apart for the rider to steer through the centre of them. Gradually move them closer and closer so the child becomes more accurate in steering and riding in a straight line.

- Two poles side by side also useful for practicing rein back.

- Place the poles randomly round the arena and time each child to trot over as many as possible in a minute. Advanced riders can canter round over them. Novices can walk over them.

- Place two poles around 10 feet apart parallel to one another in two areas of the arena. You turn your back while the children walk or trot around the arena passing through the trot poles (actually the poles are a river). When you turn around whichever pony and rider are in the river are out of the game. This is more fun played with music. Turn off the music and whoever is in the river is out.

- Poles can be placed in such a way as to create a maze. The children weave in and out of the maze on their pony.

- Poles can be used to practice road sense in the safety of the school before venturing out onto the road. Place the poles in such a way as they become road junctions etc. Also include the children using hand signals at the junctions.

Introducing the Child to Jumps

The pony that is used to teach jumping must of course be able to jump. The pony must be very free moving over the jumps and able to bascule correctly. The bascule is the nice round shape that a jumping pony should make as opposed to the hollow shape that many adopt over a fence. The pony should be able to jump a small fence without a change in pace or rhythm. It is no good attempting to teach a child to jump on a pony that is not confident himself. Nor must you consider using a pony that refuses easily or jumps a lot higher than the fence requires.

Make sure that the obstacles to be jumped during the first lesson are familiar to the pony. Sometimes when jumping new previously un- jumped fences, even the best jumping pony may over react or jump a bit higher than normal.

When giving any type of jumping lesson make sure that the pony and rider are well worked in. Usually jumping is performed after the pony has been warmed up and put through his basic paces. The pony should be moving forward with a good amount of impulsion. A forward going pony will produce a much more fluent jump that a sluggish pony. This will help with rider balance.

Teaching children to jump must be approached in a methodical and careful manner. Some children take to jumping quickly and some children absolutely hate it. You must never force a child to jump if they do not wish to. As with any pace of riding you must not pressurise a child to advance and you must go with the needs of the child. It is important to encourage but never to insist.

Sometimes a child will attempt things you suggest to them as they want to please the instructor. However there are times when you must make it clear that they do not have to do anything they are not happy with. If you are in tune with your riders you will often be able to pick up subtle signals from the child which indicates they are hiding their fear from you. This is why I believe you cannot be a good children's instructor unless you truly like children. If you are teaching children because you have to then you will not be in tune with them.

Discuss, with a demonstration from an experienced rider, the jumping position and why it is necessary.

Jumping position;

- Shorten the stirrups by 1-2 holes
- Lean forward with riders chest towards ponies crest
- Lower leg remains still with heels deep
- The rider must slide their bottom to the back of the saddle and raise it out of the saddle
- The rider holds a chunk of mane or the neck strap (some children are frightened to hold the mane for fear they will hurt the pony, you must explain that the pony will not feel them holding a thick chunk of the mane).

Why is it Necessary?

- The rider adopts this position to remain with the pony's centre of gravity.
- This position will help keep the rider balanced and stable.

- It makes jumping easier for the pony and rider.
- Takes some of the riders weight off the ponies back

Firstly practice the jumping position at a stand still. Then send the children off round the arena. First in walk then in trot have the children adopting jumping position along the short side of the arena. Place out the trotting poles and instruct the children to trot over the poles in their jumping position. Practice this and correct any positional faults that occur. After trotting over poles in the jumping position place the last two poles as a small cross. Instruct the child to hold the neck strap as he approaches the cross. The child should hardly notice that a jump has been performed. It is wise to stay at this level for a couple of weeks before raising the jump. A good foundation will be developed by building the child's confidence over small fences. To add variety you can introduce one or two more small crosses around the arena. Even when you begin to raise the fence it would be beneficial to use cross fences. A cross will not only encourage pony and rider to the centre but the jump will also be fluent. Straight bar jumps must only be introduced when the rider is established over the cross and in all paces.

Make sure that positional faults are corrected regularly. The most common faults are;

- Heels up with toes vertical to the floor
- Getting left behind
- Staying in the forward position too long
- Lower leg swinging back towards the flank area
- Looking down at the ground
- Round shoulders

- Dropping the pony at the fence by releasing the contact

Although at a more advanced stage a serious fault is catching the pony in the mouth with the reins and bit. Such a fault should not occur at this stage as, until balance is established over the fences, a novice child will be holding the neck strap/mane at all times!

Use of School Movements

Children love to learn new things! They love to feel when reaching the end of the lesson that they have achieved something new. School movements add variety for both pony and rider. They also provide stimulation and new challenges. These movements also get the riders away from the arena fence which in itself can be a daunting prospect. The fence of the arena provides a feeling of security and it is easy to become attached to it. Riding around the outside of the school is easy for both the pony and the rider. Once they start to perform school movements' things become a little more difficult.

You must explain to the children that the work they are about to embark on will be a little more demanding. It is better to forewarn them so that they are aware and do not feel they are failing if it goes wrong. They need to know that they will have to work a little harder to achieve good results.

For simple school movements I like to include:

- Twenty metre circles

- Serpentine of three to four loops
- Shallow loops
- Turn about the forehand to the left and right
- Figure of eight

You can introduce more at a later date but I find these are ideal for the children and they seem to find them easy to perform. You must talk them through each exercise clearly and precisely. I usually will either walk round in front explaining to the children as we go. If I have leaders available they will walk as I teach. It is important that you stress what they are doing and why?

Twenty Metre Circles are a rider's introduction to the many circles they will ride in the future. Children love to learn about the tangent points (the four furthest points of the circle) and enjoy shouting "tangent points" upon reaching each one. Explain the positioning of the riders legs on the circles and how they must position the pony. Also making sure that upon reaching the tangent point they must look ahead to the next tangent point.

At this stage the children do seem to learn about the aids for a circle well. Explain about the inside leg being at the girth and the outside leg behind the girth. Tell the children why? Explaining that a pony prefers to go straight as opposed to bending around the inside leg. This is why we place the outside leg back behind the girth so that the pony does not straighten himself up as soon as we ask him to bend. Talk also about the need to squeeze the inside rein to flex the pony to the inside.

The serpentine is a very beneficial exercise for both pony and rider. Such exercises are introduced at walk; this also gives the pony a rest from the faster work. The exercise will supple the pony while the rider is improving co-ordination and application of the aids.

The serpentine can be performed in three or four loops (you can actually do as many loops as you like once the rider is skilled). It is important to discuss the exercise as the child rides it. You must insist that the circular sections are ridden correctly with the proper bend and that the straight bits are, just that, straight. The reason being is the regular change of bends and the straightening of the pony increases the suppleness and obedience. This also will improve co-ordination of the children riding. Children seem to learn these moves quickly and will eventually perform them very well if trained correctly. If children forget from week to week what the serpentine exercise is I usually term it as the squiggly one.

Shallow loops are always ridden with great pride by children I have taught. Again they have a feeling of achievement when learning new exercises. You, as the instructor, must insist on the correct riding of the figures. Explain why the loops are beneficial and explain how they must be ridden. You must emphasise the changes of bend as this is the most beneficial part of the exercise. The child's co-ordination will also benefit from this work. If you have a large riding area the children can build up to performing two shallow loops down each side. Each loop will be smaller in order to fit them in. But the smaller shallow loops will benefit pony and rider. The pony will increase suppleness and the rider will become more capable of bending the pony and precision of the aids to ask for the bends.

To ride the shallow loop the rider must ride the pony round the outside track of the school. Ride the first corner of the school deep with the aids for the corner. Let's imagine we are riding a shallow loop on the left rein. Ride deep into the left corner with the left leg at the girth and the right leg behind. The pony must be slightly bent to the left. The rider must then bring the pony off the track and ride a shallow loop. The loop is very important as when riding the loop the rider must change the bend of the pony. So as we are on the left rein the pony must change to a right bend on the shallow loop. Once the rider and pony have completed the loop then they must start to return to the track just before the second corner. It is then time to change the bend back yet again to a left bend. Remember, it is the change of bends that provides the most benefit to both pony and rider.

You will need to recap in future lessons as the school movements do need to become a regular part of training. The children sometimes forget the names of the movements. Jog their memories by using simple terms, for example using the term banana exercise to remind them of the shallow loop!

Turn about the forehand is a slightly more difficult exercise for a child to learn. This exercise will need to be recapped on a regular basis until it is second nature. This exercise gives the ideal opportunity for the instructor to educate the child regarding turning a pony around without pulling at its mouth. I notice many riders, when asked to walk forward after a short interval, will simply take hold of one rein and screw the poor pony round on the spot. One of my pet hates I am afraid to say. This always looks so uncomfortable for the pony. A rider should be told to either walk forward before the turn or perform a correct turn, such as, a turn on the forehand!

Yet again always try and keep it simple for the child. Walking forward they should begin to slow the pony down to, almost, a standstill. Then when the pony is almost stopped they should bring back the leg to push the quarters in the direction they wish to turn. So if we wish them to turn right the rider must;

- Ask for the pony to slow right down to almost a halt
- Squeeze the right rein so the pony flexes right
- Take the right leg behind the girth and nudge the pony around the pivot of his own front legs.

Simple really especially when you known how! This is a much kinder way to turn the pony and removes the need for the children to drag them around by the bit. Once the rider has practiced the turn about the forehand a couple of times they must then trot the pony around the arena. Turn about the forehand can leave the horse lacking in impulsion. A good trot round should restore the impulsion quickly.

The benefits of this exercise are;

- Obedience
- Helps to supple the pony
- Rider co-ordination of aids
- Makes turning easier
- The ability to manoeuvre opening gates when the child gets older
- First introduction to lateral work

Figure of Eight is a fairly simple exercise and should be taught as two twenty metre circles with a couple of straight strides to separate the two circles. This needs to be taught early as it is required for any riding classes in the future. Always make sure circles are ridden in a good shape with the correct aids used. The tangent points can be used as spoke about earlier. The tangent points will help make the circle a good shape.

Chapter 4 Teaching Stable Management

Stable management is a vital aspect of teaching any rider and must not be neglected. In very bad weather if you do not have an indoor school this would be an ideal time to cover some stable management. However if you are lucky enough to have an indoor school then you will need to incorporate stable management into your schedule at some stage. Some schools provide 4/5 weeks riding lessons with every sixth week being a compulsory stable management session. I think this can work well as stable management is so important for the rider.

Children love to learn as much as they can about the ponies they are riding. They seem to soak up knowledge very readily. Keep lessons fairly basic to begin with and keep the fun element intact at all times.

Whichever pony you decide to use for practical stable management must be a very reliable pony. You must certainly never consider using a pony that kicks or bites. The pony must be placid and enjoy being surrounded by young children. There are not many ponies out there which do not enjoy standing around being fussed. As you may have to tie your pony up for long periods during these lessons, a full hay net will keep him occupied. I have often seen ponies falling into a deep relaxed state when being handled and groomed by children! This is so wonderful to see. The first picture below shows just that!

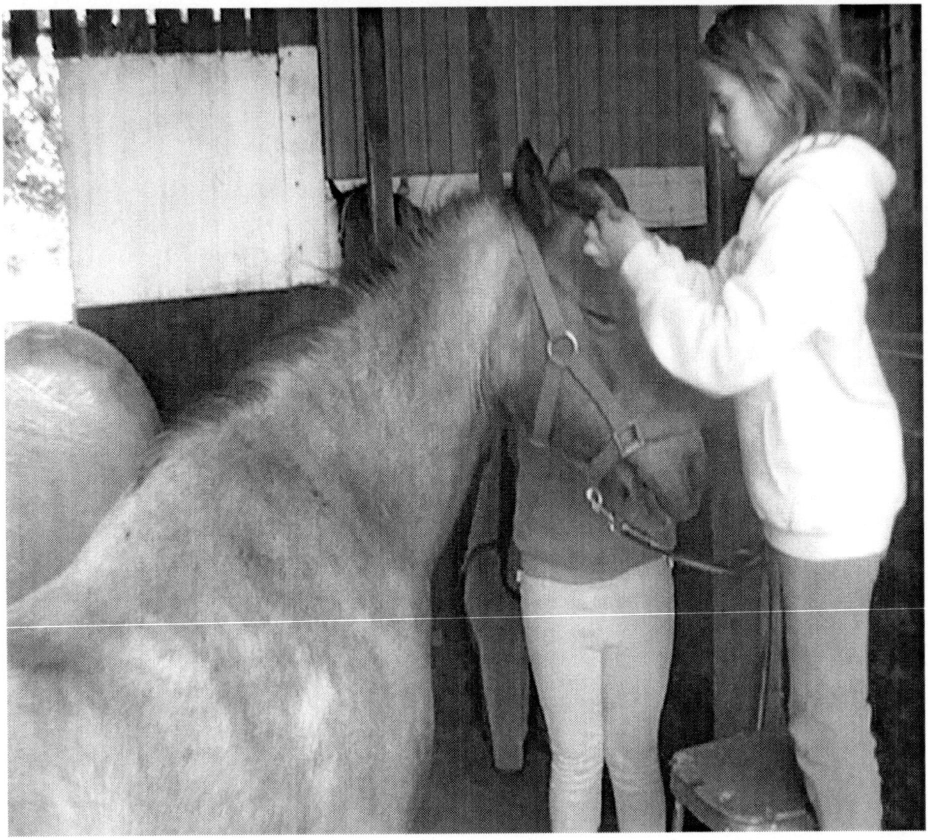

Kids just love to be with ponies

The stable management lessons can be performed in a stable or barn. You can have a very quiet pony available for practical work that involves being around or handling a pony. Tacking up can be practised also as can mucking out and setting fair the stable. Grooming is also very popular with children as it is something they can do easily. Make sure that you have all your equipment to hand so that you are not popping in and out of the stable. In order to be safe the pony must of course be tied up securely and with a quick release knot. When tying up ponies the children must not only learn the quick release knot but they must also be made aware of the danger caused by tying ponies to fixed objects. Show them the importance of tying a piece of baler twine to the tie ring. Then tie the pony to the baler twine. If the pony gets frightened and pulls away at least he will not be fixed to a solid unyielding object that will cause him to injure himself. The baler twine should break in an emergency and this will prevent injury to the pony.

On a summer day, when the sun is shining, it is wonderful to take the children and ponies out of the stable onto the yard to perform grooming, handling, points of the pony etc. It is also a great benefit to escort the children around the paddocks to discuss paddock management with them.

Remember all the safety rules of being around the ponies even if they are not being ridden. Make sure all the children have their hard riding hats on even when they are on the ground. Gloves must be worn for any leading. If a pony decides to run away from a child while being led a rope burn can easily occur if gloves are not worn. Always remind the children to walk around the front of the pony and to behave in a calm and quiet manner.

One thing I have concluded in my years teaching child riders, they simply like to be with ponies. Most of all they like the physical contact of the pony. No matter what lessons I plan for them during stable management children simply want to be with ponies!

Early Stable Management

With very small children I would usually consider points of the horse to be a good starting point. There are so many simple parts of the pony that children can learn very easily. Here are some further ideas for early management lessons.

- Tying up safely (quick release knot)
- Picking out the feet and looking at the parts of the foot (frog)
- Bandaging tails and legs
- Grooming the pony and names of the brushes
- Basic rules of feeding
- Parts of the saddle and bridle
- Tacking up the pony
- Filling hay nets
- How to spot a healthy/unhealthy pony (keep it basic)
- Leading a pony correctly and safely (kids love this)
- Mucking out and setting fair
- Basic points of the pony

The above are just suggestions; you need to consider age and development of the children you are teaching. Some may not be able to handle a bridle or manage a quick release knot so you will have to use your common sense and judgement. Do bear in mind that children are quick to learn. Many small children are capable of tacking up and more. They just need to be encouraged with patience and understanding. Practice, practice and practice some more.

Introduce children early on to approach a pony safely as they will need to do this often. Point out about the blind spots and make sure they are aware of these. Encourage them to talk to the pony as they approach.

Build on the stable management lessons throughout the child's career; as they develop you can develop the lessons accordingly. I have found that children will certainly take in theory well at a young age, especially if you repeat lessons regularly. Also incorporate stable management into your riding lessons. For example you can discuss points of the pony when having a breather during a lesson. You can ask the child parts of the saddle when walking round the arena. It is a matter of repetition on a regular basis to make sure that it all becomes second nature.

Children love pointing out parts of the pony while they are riding. Games can be played in the arena involving for example;

- Racing to a bucket of grooming brushes, dismount pick a brush run back on foot and discuss the brush and what its use is.

- Racing to a bucket of grooming brushes and picking out a particular brush as instructed.

- Walking or trotting to one end of the arena and being asked a question about ponies. The rider cannot go back to the finish line until they answer a question.

- The instructor asks each child in turn to name a point of the pony

- Simon says is a good game to play e.g. Simon says touch the ponies poll/dock etc

Just use your imagination and use every opportunity possible to educate the rider.

Written Work for the Child

Children do love to draw or write during stable management lessons. They love to draw horses and mark out basic points. And they love to answer questions in written form.

Children also love to be presented with pictures and written pieces that they need to fill in the missing words or write down the name of parts of the pony etc. Occasionally there may not always be time to cover as much as you would like. In such an instance you can send the child home with work to do. I have noticed children get great enjoyment out of this. They also like to go away with some work to learn. They love to return for the following lesson and answer questions on the homework. This works particularly well with small groups of children. The competitive spirit soon kicks in and children seem to become very enthusiastic during such work.

Children love doing quizzes and showing off their new found knowledge. If you have time at the end of a session it is good to produce the children with a simple quiz covering what they have learned. You have to be very careful that all the children can read and write to roughly the same level. For this reason I often put the children in pairs or teams.

Question Time

Once the stable management session is completed it is helpful to hold a discussion covering the work done during the lesson. Ask simple questions making sure that all the children get the chance to answer at least one each. You may find that some children are over eager and tend to try and answer all the questions. To prevent this I will usually ask the children to put their hand in the air if they know the answer. If you notice a child that is unable to answer a question try and think of really simple ones to help build up confidence.

Use of Visual Aids

Whenever I have taken part in any learning experience my favourite sections have always been the visual bits. I suppose I personally learn better from visual aids but I also find it more interesting and stimulating. Something to look at/feel/touch adds to the interest. Such aids seem to help a lesson ingrain a little better into the brain.

When teaching about feeds it is helpful to have a variety of different feedstuffs in little jars. You can label them and they keep for a long time. Collect as many horsy items together so that as you teach about the items, you can hand them round for inspection by the pupils.

A collection of different protective boots is handy to have. This can help towards a very interesting lecture on the use and variety of boots and other protection for the pony. The children can also attempt to put the different types of boots on a quiet pony. A selection of bandages also benefits. There are so many different types on the market these days. Just have the basic bandages for the tail, legs and stable bandages.

A collection of shoes and bits is ideal. Handing round the items and discussing their uses is invaluable learning for the child. If you are lucky enough to get hold of remedial shoes they can stimulate interesting discussions between your pupils.

Again the possibilities are endless and the imagination needs to be employed. What may seem uninteresting to you will be new and interesting to your young pupils. Try and put yourself into their shoes and think about how new and exciting everything is to them.

Getting to Know Ponies

It is important that children learn as much as they can about the ponies they ride. Not just how to make them walk and trot or how to put a saddle on. Children need to learn that ponies have strong feelings just like they do. They need to learn that ponies are not machines that do everything they are told. Ponies have good days and bad days just like humans. If children are made aware of the feelings and behaviour of ponies early in their career it will help them to become more compassionate riders for the future.

Stable management sessions therefore should include behaviour of the pony. A session could consist of a relaxed hour in the fields observing the ponies in their own environment. Children will benefit from watching ponies interact with one another. During such sessions, grazing, water and fencing etc can be discussed. There can be no prediction of what a group of ponies will show you during an hour's observation. You may be very lucky and see the following

- Mutual grooming

- Ponies in conflict
- Rolling
- Playtime
- Sleeping
- Courtship
- Friendships
- Pair bonds

Each and every activity the pony displays will bring about the chance to educate. Grasp everything the ponies show you and discuss it with the children. Even bad behaviour during observation can lead to interesting discussions. Enjoying observing the ponies will bring about more understanding from the children. This can only help towards the child and pony relationship that we must encourage and nurture.

Poisonous Plants

It would be beneficial to talk about poisonous plants although hopefully you will not have any in the paddock to show the children! It would be a good idea to have pictures of the worst plants and of course no doubt there will be some infamous Ragwort on grass verges where you are. Ragwort is abundant around the countryside and the children must be informed of the seriousness surrounding this plant. This plant can also affect human health and the child needs to be aware not to touch it without gloves and long sleeves covering their arms.

Ragwort must be removed by adults wearing gloves. A Ragwort fork can be purchased and these are excellent at removing the whole root and make the job a lot easier. Once the ragwort is pulled from the ground it really should be burnt or disposed of well such as green bins etc. There must not be any remains of the plant whatsoever. Please be aware that Ragwort is even more palatable when it is dead and dry!

If eaten this plant can destroy the kidneys of the ponies and also, when breathed in, the pollen is dangerous too.

Ragwort in its early stages known as the rosette stage

Ragwort is not the only poison plant, there are many. Some examples are;

- Privet
- Foxglove

- Aconite
- Deadly Nightshade
- Hemlock
- Laburnum
- Yew
- Bracken
- Ivy

Chapter 5 Having Fun on Ponies

Bring Fun into Riding

Riding for children and adults should involve an element of fun. However for child riders it is even more important. Children can learn so much by having fun and this element can also make the rider forget any worries or fears they may have about riding ponies.

Children are naturally competitive; this can be used to the advantage of the instructor. If you have a small group of children you can then introduce fun competitions to enable the competitive spirit to help towards their training.

If you teach your rider on a one to one basis then you will need to cal on some little helpers. You can still organise races between the child on the pony and the little helpers. Make sure the little helpers are kept safe and the races are not to fast.

Games to play

Gymkhana games are always very popular especially at a young age. There are so many games to choose from and children generally do enjoy all of them. If you have a good imagination you can even make up your own games. Ponies do tend to pick up on the excitement and anticipation of fun lessons. Make sure that the leaders are aware and stop any ponies getting too excited. Try and keep every child safe to the best of your ability.

Races are very good as they are in a straight line thus balance is not disturbed too much. At the early stage of the child's career canter is best kept out of the races. When the competitive spirit shines through you will notice a definite boldness develop so proceed with caution to keep your little riders safe. Such games and races will encourage better reactions from the rider and they hopefully will forget all their anxieties.

Suggested Races

Walk and trot race is so simple; the riders walk to one end of the arena and trot back. If any rider breaks pace (trotting when they should be walking etc) the pony and rider must turn a circle. When the child has learnt to canter this can be included in the race.

You can add many combinations to this race such as;

- The rider walks the pony to the end and does 'around the world' before heading back.

- The rider walks or trots the pony to one end of the arena, dismounts and runs back on foot. Make sure the leader holds the pony while the rider runs back!

- The rider walks to the end dismounts and jumps a fence on their way to the winning line. With more experienced children they can jump the fence while riding the pony.

- The rider walks or trots to one end and has to bring a piece of horsy equipment back from a box they must name the article and explain its use. This works well with grooming brushes, boots etc. Obviously you must have already taught the child about the items!

- The rider can get a piece of clothing off a specially constructed wash line and put it on before racing back to the winning line.

- Walk, trot, canter and lead is more advanced but great fun. Walk up, trot down, canter up and then get off and lead your pony back.

Sack Race is a very physical and testing race that is great fun to play. Hessian sacks are usually the best and can be obtained by asking your local post master! Sometimes they will give you old bags. The children will ride as fast as they can to the sacks and then dismount. Leaders will take the ponies while the children get in the sacks and jump back to the start.

Musical Sacks Another good use for Hessian sacks. Put the sacks in a circle in the middle of the arena spaced out evenly. The children ride around them until the music stops. Once the music stops the children dismount, the leaders hold the pony and the children run and jump on a sack. Remove a sack leaving one short and the rider who fails to get a sack is out. This can be played with more experienced children and in this case (provided all ponies are friendly to each other) the children run to the sack with their pony.

Egg and spoon race is great fun but make sure the eggs are hard boiled. We often play this game with a cream egg. The kids love this idea as they get to eat the egg. Again there are different ideas for this simple race.

- Egg and spoon performed completely from start to finish while riding the pony.

- The child can ride to one end of the arena, dismount and race back with the egg and spoon. This is usually so funny to watch and the children soon learn how to balance the egg while running.

Dressing up Race This is one of my all time favourite races. The props are easy to get hold of from your wardrobe. If you don't have any old clothes I am sure you will be able to get hold of some from a jumble sale or similar. The children have to race to the end of the arena, dismount, and get dressed into the clothes you have placed there. They then re-mount and race back to the start. This game usually causes lots of fun and laughter and always brightens my day.

You can adapt this game depending on the ability of the riders. The clothes can be placed on a washing line and the child has to remove them from the wash line while on or off the pony again depending on the ability and of course, suitability of the pony. They then dress up, race to the other end, then back again to replace the washing on the line.

Bending races are fun and very educational. You are getting two things for the price of one. The pony gets suppling exercises and the rider practices steering without even being aware of the work they are doing. You can use traffic cones or any other fairly large items for the children to weave in and out of.

Traffic Lights
- The red light is halt

- Yellow light is walk
- Green light is trot or canter (depending on rider experience)

The instructor or helper has to stand at one end of the arena while the ponies and riders head towards them. The instructor holds up a coloured card and the riders must change pace accordingly. The last one to make the change of pace is out. You must insist that aids are correct and not harsh in any way.

Water Ride Each rider is given a full cup of water. They must ride at a certain pace while keeping as much water in the cup as possible. Who ever has the most water at the end is the winner. Make sure the weather is not too cold for this race.

Tacking up race This can be varied as the children can begin with the ponies tacked up. Ride to the opposite end of the arena and remove the saddle. Remount (with assistance) and ride back to the other end. Then return at the pace chosen by the instructor and place the saddle back on and ride to the finish line.

Musical ride I think it is always a nice change to bring a bit of music into riding. This game involves a good portable stereo and some peaceful music (no heavy metal etc). Horses and ponies have been found to enjoy a bit of classical music. The riders are instructed to go at a given pace until the music stops. Once the music stops the ponies must be stopped, the last one to halt is out. Again you must make sure the riders don't get rough in order to halt the pony. The aids must be applied kindly as ever they should be.

Handy Pony although not a race this game is great fun. The instructor can let their imagination run wild. If you have ever seen handy pony at local shows you will notice the many children clambering to get in and have a go. My niece and her pony used to be handy pony queens. That was little Dancer I mentioned early on in the book. She was so talented in the handy pony ring. Even the children can become involved in helping you design a course. Here are some ideas but the possibilities are endless;

- A big bell for the children to ring while mounted
- A gate to open and shut while on their pony
- Bending in and out of cones
- Stuffed bodies to ride over (scarecrows)
- Trot poles
- Two poles side by side for the rider to halt in
- Letter box with letter to post
- Removing washing from the wash line or pegging it on the line
- Dismount pick up a bean bag and mount again ride to a bucket put bean bag in
- Dismount and lead pony while going over stepping stones

You can simply let your imagination, and that of the children, run riot when thinking up obstacles and challenges. Of course you must always keep every activity as safe as possible!

Touch and out This game can be adapted for the different abilities. The idea is for the rider to take the ponies over a jump and then some drums. The drums are laid flat and in a long row. Each time the rider clears both obstacles a drum is removed and the jump is raised. With the novice children just the row of drums can be used. The children ride over the drums and one is removed each time. Eventually there will only be one or two drums to jump and this will prove difficult.

Simon Says This seems to be very popular with children and they love to listen out for Simon's next task. This game is ideal when a rider needs to be distracted quickly if the pony has upset them in any way. Again you could incorporate touching pony body parts at Simon's request.

Grandma's Footsteps is a simple but enjoyable game for the kids. The instructor or a volunteer walks in front of the ponies and the children walk their ponies behind the person who plays Grandma. Each time Grandma stops and looks round the riders must be motionless. Whoever moves is out of the game.

Exercise on the Pony

Exercises performed while riding are very beneficial for a variety of reasons;

- Supples the rider
- Variety
- Balance
- Builds confidence
- Slow work for interludes
- Warming up and cooling down

If you have specific problems then there are exercises to help. You can also use your imagination to come up with your own exercises.

If you are working with a group then use a lead rider to simply ride at the front, keeping the pace at the required speed. This is particularly useful if you take away the reins and knot them. This will also be useful if you take away stirrups also. It is not advisable to remove both at the same time.

Removing the stirrups is a useful exercise as the child will develop a deeper seat and the balance will improve. The rider will also gain confidence in their own ability. It is wise to embark upon such exercise with a leader to start with.

Stiffness in the Ankle area

Take away the riders stirrups and instruct them to walk the pony around. As they do so they must rotate the ankle clockwise and anticlockwise. The effect of this is usually instant and the ankle can be seen to be much more soft and supple. This exercise is excellent for dancers who ride as well. I have had many riders with ankle and toe issues whose hobbies include dancing. Dancers are trained to use their ankles to support various dance moves. This seems to require a strong rigid ankle and this is where their problem arises. Horse riding requires a soft supple ankle and this exercise will help. Perform the rotations several times each way.

Stiffness in the Neck and Shoulder Area

A simple exercise for this problem is to ask the rider to bring their shoulders up to their ears. They need to hold this for a couple of seconds and then relax. This can be done several times with the effects normally instant. Also looking sideways left and right will loosen neck muscles. Make sure the movement is performed slowly and carefully.

Touching Toes This is a confidence builder and will help supple the waist area. Also, done correctly, the rider will be encouraged to lean forward while keeping the leg in the correct position.

A similar exercise will be asking the child to touch various pony body parts. Obviously the parts must be reachable. It would be no good asking the rider to touch the chestnut! Suitable areas will be as follows.

- Poll
- Dock
- Withers
- Shoulder
- Crest
- Ears
- Mane
- Loins

The above would also prove to be educational as the child will become very familiar with the various parts over time.

Riding out in open spaces

This is great fun for any age of rider. However riding their ponies in large open spaces can be a daunting experience for the child. Over the years I have had various reactions from children when venturing into the fields. Reactions range from tears to laughter. Children sometimes have such fun they want to go on and on. Occasionally children do pick up on the extra impulsion generated by entering a field. It can feel frightening and the child may lose nerve completely. This of course must be respected as no child must ever be persuaded to face situations before they feel ready. I can assure you that when the time is right for the rider it will happen.

Nothing beats riding across fields and meadows

It is a new feeling for children to experience. The ponies will be on their toes and anticipating a good run. Therefore it is important that you only use the most reliable of ponies. And of course the children, for the first few outdoor sessions, are on the lead rein.

If a pony is prone to getting over excited then you would be better not to use such ponies. Only the most quiet and most reliable will do. Only use the most efficient of your leaders to do the field work.

Start the session by walking around the field in order to settle both pony and rider. Gradually work up to a steady trot. It is important to assess the behaviour of pony and rider to consider if it is safe to finish on a short canter. If carried out safely and efficiently you will probably find children will be begging to return to the field in the future. Keep this work as a periodic treat for the riders.

Bareback Riding

Bareback riding is beneficial in many ways,

- Pony and Rider are in closer physical contact
- Rider becomes more aware of the movement of the pony
- Balance of the rider improves
- Confidence of the rider will grow
- Deeper seat will become evident
- Great fun for the rider
- Relaxing and comfortable for the pony

Bareback riding can be offered to the children as a change from the normal routine. This will add a new dimension to their riding skills. Some ponies are more comfortable than others for bareback riding. This needs to be bourn in mind when planning the session and what paces will be carried out.

One pony will be suitable for all paces while another may only be suitable for walking. The type of work undertaken during a bareback session will depend on the competence of the rider. With beginners they can work at just walking and steering. A more advanced rider can work at all paces and possibly even jumping.

Children love to do exercises while riding bareback. They enjoy the warmth of the close contact with the pony. They can feel each and every move the pony makes. Ask the children to lie back completely and relax as the pony is lead round. Ask them to close their eyes and just trust in the pony and leader. Ask them to lean forward and totally embrace the pony as they are lead round. Then ask them to do around the world but stop half way. As they are sat facing their ponies hind quarters get them to lay forward again with their head on the hind quarters. Eyes closed again as they are lead round the arena. At the end of this type of session you should find the children become very chilled out and relaxed.

As with any advancement in the child's skills during riding, the work must be built up slowly. Competent leaders will be able to stop the pony immediately should difficulty become evident. Remember that work without a saddle will be demanding on the leg muscles. The legs will be hanging longer and more effort will be required to stay on board. This can leave the children with sore muscles. If they are not sore on the day of the lesson they will be the next day.

I usually embark on bareback riding half way through a lesson. The kids usually enjoy un-tacking the pony themselves. This obviously is good practice and must be carried out correctly. When the session ends it is also good practice for the children to tack up the pony again before returning him to the stable.

Hacking out with the Ponies

Hacking out with small children is very beneficial to all concerned. It gives everyone a breath of fresh air and is a good rest from the working environment of the arena.

The ponies become lively with excitement as, they too, love to leave the confines of the arena. The instructor benefits also from this delightful change of routine. Make sure you only take the children out in very good weather. Rain and wind in particular can upset ponies thus upsetting the children.

The ponies hacking out must be absolutely bomb proof in all situations. They should be experienced at going out on the roads and lanes. The ponies must be well behaved no matter what hazards they come across. Tractors, livestock, bikes, pushchairs to name but a few hazards you may encounter on rides. Nobody can ever predict fully what you may meet or the behaviour of the pony; this is why it is vital to have lead reins and very experienced leaders.

When hacking out on the lead rein make sure that you never use a quick release or safety lead rope. These, I consider, to be a very dangerous piece of equipment. They can easily come undone leaving a rider very vulnerable. If a pony plays up and gets away the consequences are unthinkable. Always use a standard and sturdy lead rope that will remain attached to the pony in all circumstances.

As an instructor it is possible to take just one child out while riding yourself. The child must of course be on the lead rein which the instructor will be holding onto. The horse ridden by the instructor must be very reliable and placid and trained to go out with a pony on the lead rein.

When leaving home/school the instructor must inform next in command of the route they plan to take and the estimated time it will take. It is sensible to carry a mobile phone for if you get into difficulty. A small first aid pack and extra lead rope should also be carried. A hoof pick will be vital; you can purchase a fold up one. You just never know when you may need to remove a stone from the pony/horse's hoof.

If you have a small group of novice children I would advise the instructor to be on foot. Each child should be on the lead rein with an experienced leader beside them. I personally like to be on foot so that I can walk up and down the group encouraging riders and possibly correcting faults. Although we are having a break from lessons I feel it is still important that the riders sit correctly and ride their ponies well. I also feel content in the knowledge that should a child become distressed or a pony become naughty I am immediately on hand to help control the situation.

The hack is an ideal situation to practice trotting as it will mostly be straight lines. The pony will probably be more forward going and have more impulsion due to the enjoyment factor. This will help the rider perform the rising trot better as the pony's rhythm will be more constant.

Hacking will also be a useful time to introduce road sense and hand signals etc. It is also important at this young age to teach the children manners and etiquette towards other road / bridle path users. Too often these days people on horseback fail to display courtesy to others enjoying the great outdoors.

Hacking can be enjoyed by all children and should be considered a great treat. I would therefore advise that it is carried out about once every 4/6 weeks. Use the time to allow the children to learn in a more relaxed environment.

While hacking out with children or adults it is vital to remember high visibility clothing. This is important so that motorists become aware of you at the earliest opportunity so they can adjust their driving accordingly. Also, if the visibility drops in situations, such as unexpected fog, you are then much more visible to drivers. The horses can be provided with high visibility exercise sheets as these are really prominent to motorists.

Hacking is yet another opportunity to instil care of the pony upon the children. They should be encouraged to walk the first five minutes and also the last five minutes. Explain that this will help keep the ponies sound in the long run by warming them up and cooling them down. Both of which are equally important.

Upon returning home the riders need to be made aware of the ponies needs. If the pony is hot and sweating then the child will need to learn about putting on the correct rug to help cool the pony safely. They can also be told to prepare a feed but not to feed until the pony is properly cooled down and his breathing has slowed to normal. If the pony is not correctly looked after when returning home then he may chill. If he is fed to soon then he may get colic. All these lessons are vital for the future of the pony and rider. During this time you can discuss proper breathing rates. The resting breathing rate for a pony is somewhere between 8-16 breaths per minute. This needs to be kept in mind when feeding a pony after work!

Children need to learn early on in their riding career that ponies can be such fun and a joy to be around. But the most important aspect of their learning must be the care and empathy for any pony they get to ride or own. They can enjoy ponies and have fun on them so long as the pony is always put first and foremost during all the fun times. Once it stops being fun for the pony it's time to call it a day and finish the ride.

Chapter 6 Holiday time On Horseback

At the farm where I teach, holiday time means exciting pony rides are on the menu. Variety is of course the spice of life and seasonal celebrations can bring a new dimension for the children and ponies. This chapter contains suggestions for different activities during the important dates on the calendar.

Christmas Tinsel Ride

I will begin with the Christmas holidays as, this to me, is the most exciting of all. Christmas, to me, means the Tinsel ride, a time when the children arrive early to prepare their pony for this important annual event.

The children can decorate their ponies as festively as they possibly can. Of course safety must still be top of the priority list. Make sure the ponies you use are able to cope with flapping tinsel and baubles. It is amazing to see what some of the kids will come up with.

Once the ponies are decorated and prepared we will go off on the tinsel ride. This usually involves a trip down the lanes with lots of smiling children. The ponies seem to enjoy this ride as much as the children. A prize can be given for the best decorated pony.

Children not only love to dress the ponies up, they like to dress up themselves. Again safety must not be forgotten just because we are having fun! Even Santa's little helper needs to wear a hard riding hat when dealing with ponies.

Pony Christmas cake competition

The children will need plenty of notice for this one and must be told at least one week in advance. The idea of the competition is to make up a cake recipe for a pony cake.

They must make the cake and bring it to the annual competition. They must also provide the recipe, so that if the ponies like it, the cake can be made by others also. The kids really enjoy making a carrot and apple based cake that the ponies will enjoy. The kids also love it when the ponies themselves judge the cake by eating it! A prize can be given to the winner that makes the most popular cake. Yes the ponies can judge the cake competition! It is amazing how they will tuck into certain cakes and turn their nose completely up at the not so nice ones.

Some of the amazing cakes that have been presented by my pupils have been outstanding. The decorations on the top ranging from sliced apples and carrots and of course, polo mints. It is obvious the enthusiasm that is brought about by the cakes when you see the results!

Easter Rides

I often take the children on a short Easter hack with a treasure hunt included. The children love finding hidden Easter eggs and sweeties with the aid of a list of clues. You should have fun with the list of clues. The clues, nothing too complicated, should guide the children towards their Easter treats. This ride will involve a lot of planning beforehand but is well worth it. The children love to compete with their peers to finding the goodies. With the list of clues and lots of hidden treasures you will need to call on all your helpers to be present. The children will have to dismount on a regular basis in order to look in hedges/behind walls etc. Make sure there are plenty of treats to go round all the kids.

The Easter treasure hunt can be organised round a big field if you have access to one. With hedges,trees, gateways and feed troughs you should have plenty of hiding places. Also the ride can be a more relaxed affair without worrying about traffic and other hazards.

Summer Holidays

Summer holidays were made for children and ponies. Many riding schools now organise *Own a Pony days*. These can work out expensive but are usually enjoyed immensely by the children. Each child is allocated a pony on arrival and that pony belongs to them for the whole day. An example time table for the day is shown.

10am Arrive and meet in tack room to be allocated a pony

10.30 Practical session mucking out their pony

11.30 Stable management points of the pony

12.30 Lunch (usually children will be asked to bring their own packed
Lunch)

1pm Tacking up their ponies

!.30 Riding lesson

2.30 Untack ponies

2.45   Pony quiz

3.30   Home time

The above is just a suggested timetable for guidance. The possibilities are endless and can be so very educational and fun at the same time. Make sure that you group the children in accordance to their ability. There is nothing worse than children being held back due to bad grouping. Also pressure is put on the less experienced riders if they are aware of their lack of ability in comparison to the others.

Proficiency Tests

Children love to be rewarded for good work; it encourages even more effort from them. What could be better than to arrange a series of tests throughout the summer with certificates along the way? They only need to be simple for the children and designed in such a way that the first one or two are easy to pass. When the children have a couple of certificates under their belt you can then raise the criteria. If the tests are too difficult initially the children may become worried and anxious. However if you make it simple to begin with the children will gain more confidence.

If you visit your nearest office supplies shop you will find that you can purchase some very nice certificates. You can then design them yourself and make them look very professional. Most children nowadays have books especially for the certificates gained at school and during after school pursuits. Pony riding certificates would sit nicely in such folders.

Make sure that the children get to practice the tests in their weekly lesson. Also it would be nice to make smart dress part of the criteria. It is never too early for children to realise the importance of presentation. Not everyone will have show clothes etc so smart dress is simply shirt and tie, clean jodhpurs. It should not include show jackets and the like as not everyone will have them.

Basic first test could consist of:

- Mounting
- Holding the reins correctly
- Sitting correctly
- Asking the pony to walk
- Asking the pony to halt
- Dismounting

A nice little certificate could be awarded for this simple test. The children will feel a real sense of achievement on working for this. You could gradually increase the criteria and by the end of the summer the children will have worked towards, and hopefully gained, a couple of certificates while improving their riding and horsemanship.

Stable management is equally as important as riding. Therefore it would be beneficial to hold test days purely for stable management and handling ponies etc. These tests could include;

- Grooming
- Mucking out
- Points of the pony
- Feeding the pony
- Tack cleaning

You could take the children into the fields to have a look around. You could discuss fencing, types of grass, good and bad grazing, water supplies and shelters. Again, just suggestions, there should never be a dull moment when teaching children.

Riding School Show

For many young riders the riding school show will be their first event. They will know the venue of course and this will help them to remain relaxed and calm. The children should be able to ride the pony of their choice for this major event.

For a school show it would be unfair to expect the parents to purchase the correct showing attire. However to make the event special you must insist the riders turn themselves and their pony out to a high standard. Most children have a blouse or shirt and probably a school tie. They can also make a special effort to clean their boots. They should be encouraged to arrive early at the school and prepare their pony too. If the weather is warm and dry then possibly the children could bath their ponies. Children just seem to love to bath ponies and make them look pretty. If the ponies are out at grass then a thorough groom and possible light sponging would be advised.

Explain to the children that if a pony is kept at grass they should not be bathed. They should not be groomed too much either. The reason for this lack of grooming and bathing is to keep the pony healthy out in the elements. By nature itself, the pony is provided with a waterproof coat.

His coat contains oils that must be left intact to keep him waterproof. If you wash or brush the oils away then the pony will lose this waterproof protection. This would leave him vulnerable to catching a chill in wet weather.

The children must also clean all their tack to the best of their ability. If you are really organised you could incorporate the preparation into own a pony day. Not all parents will be able to afford to send their children to pony days and then a show next day. Some parents may not be able to afford two consecutive days, do bear this in mind when organising your schedule.

It would be sensible not to judge the school show yourself. Ask a knowledgeable friend to do this. Keep the schedule simple and basic to include best turned out, best ridden and a little bit of jumping. If time permits some games could be included. Fancy dress gives a rather grand finale and a nice end to the day.

Summer Camp/sleepovers at the stables

Most kids love the idea of camping or sleeping over at the riding school. It will all depend on the ages of the children as some may be a little too young. However children of 10 and over seem able to cope very well. Camping would need to be well organised with plenty of adult helpers. The event could run similarly to the own a pony days but with lots more time. A lot of camps are organised in such a way that there is a lot of outside activities such as bowling and swimming etc. I think if it's a pony camp then time should be spent with and around the ponies. Ponies all day and Supper around the camp fire is surely what riding school /pony club camps are all about!

The camp or sleep over could include lessons in all areas of horsemanship and management. Children must be encouraged to be independent but must also be protected and cared for. They must be made aware that having a go at things is important but they should feel safe in the knowledge that help is on hand.

All the work covered during the camp could culminate in quizzes and a possible show on the final day. Make sure that everyone goes home having enjoyed their time with you. If you are giving out awards, certificates and rosettes make sure that no child goes home empty handed.

Chapter 7 Further Development

The Pony Club

The Pony Club is a wonderful organisation for the development of the child rider. By contacting the head office of this organisation you will be able to source your nearest group. Joining the group local to your home will mean that the rallies and meetings etc will not be to far away.

The Pony Club is certainly value for money and the organisation can advance children remarkably well. I think its success with riders is for the following reasons;

- Children learning with peers
- Comradeship/friendship
- Structure
- Working towards goals (pony club tests)
- Possibility of riding for teams
- Regular holiday meets and rallies
- Independence
- Varied Instructors
- Variety
- Ponies get to socialise and become more worldly

The Pony Club is well structured and sorts groups out in age and ability. In a riding school environment, children can sometimes be held back. Often new riders will join a school group and the whole group has to step back to the new rider's level. This can sometimes slow the advancement of the rider. The Pony Club will asses the rider on entry. This enables groups of the same standards to be formed. I have seen it work very well. Children enjoy keeping up with one another during the learning experience. Also the competitive spirit kicks in even more.

Strong friendships can develop during day long rallies and Pony Club camps. The riders will meet regularly on horseback and with the many social gatherings that the Pony Club organises friendships are formed. Team work also helps with development of friendships as the riders will work towards badges and tests together.

The Pony Club is structured with a series of tests worked towards regularly. The tests are excellent as they start with a very basic D test which is very simple to pass. The final test is A which is considered a prestigious award to gain. The tests are designed to build ability and set standards that will benefit the rider throughout their future careers.

Before taking the C test the Riding and Road Safety Certificate must be gained. The riding and road safety is an excellent qualification to gain. This qualification will benefit the child when they venture out hacking alone or with their peers.

The Pony Club also works children towards badges. The badges are sewn onto the pony club sweatshirt. The badges don't just cover pony related topics. Topics covered are various, including farming, birds, human first aid and many more.

The Pony Club certainly does bring out the horseperson in a child. Many top riders in the country today started their early careers at the Pony Club. That speaks volumes and is well worth thinking about. The Pony Club headquarters is based in Stoneleigh, Warwickshire but has local branches all over the country. Many riding schools and hunts are affiliated to Pony Clubs, making them accessible to all areas.

Local Shows and Riding Clubs advertise their events in the local press and saddle shops. The local shows are the first step towards a competing career. You may have to pay a yearly fee and fees for each of the classes that the child enters. Most local riding clubs are unaffiliated and are run by local horsy adults. They are usually friendly meetings and last the whole day. Most riding clubs and local shows are run throughout the summer months. Often the premises are rented land/fields which are very basic.

These types of events will introduce the child to the various disciplines. The schedules are designed to have a class to appeal to all riders present. This would be a typical schedule:

- Best turned out
- Best Ridden
- First ridden (riders just off lead rein)
- Lead rein ridden (tiny tots)
- Beginners jumping
- Fledgling working hunter (tiny tots)-cradle/ nursery stakes
- Equitation

In Hand classes

- Prettiest mare
- Prettiest gelding
- Bonny pony

- Veteran
- Mountain and Moorland
- Child handler

The above are just a small selection of classes available. From this you can see that there is a class to suit every pony. It is lovely to see children flitting from class to class in order to gain their rosettes. The beauty of these shows is that they are non professional. This allows the rider to develop in either showing, jumping or in hand. Hopefully by the end of the first season the child will have decided which discipline they would like to specialise in.

The rules of these shows are not so stringent. When a child has a problem i.e. in the jumping ring, the stewards will usually help the rider to complete the course or at least the problem fences they may have encountered. After judging of the ridden classes riders often receive helpful feedback from the judge.

The child handler class is an excellent class and children love it. The class puts priority on safe handling of the ponies which is of course paramount.

Depending on the age of the child or children taking part in the shows supervision is important. The children at this stage do need to be encouraged to be independent but this must be worked towards slowly and thoughtfully. Many children get so carried away by the show they will forget to eat. More seriously they will probably forget that the pony will need refreshment throughout the day. Water must be offered frequently in small amounts and a lunch hour for both parties must be included. Do make sure that the pony has shelter from the sun or even the cold and wet, all can be equally distressing when at a show.

Also the instructor/ parent must make sure the pony gets suitable rest from carrying the rider. Many children, and their parents, think it is acceptable to sit on their ponies from 9am until the end of the show. This must not be allowed. There is nothing worse that seeing a child waiting at the ringside all day sat on a pony! It is a great strain on a pony to be stood still for long periods with a rider on board.

When first embarking on the competitive ladder, do begin very locally. Local shows have a little bit of everything so that the child can try different areas of showing. The local show usually takes membership fees and if the child goes to regular shows then they might even get a mention at the yearly awards ceremony. Points are awarded throughout the show season at local shows. If you join the club and regularly attend shows, your loyalty may result in a prize at the end of the season.

If the child attempts each class throughout the show season he will probably, by the end of the first season, find that there is one discipline he likes most of all. This discipline should be the one that the child then concentrates on for the following season, so that the chosen discipline will be perfected even more.

Handy Pony

This section of the show is normally open all day and you simply pop across and join the queue to have a go. The handy pony is a type of obstacle course that involves all sorts of little tests for the pony and rider. I have mentioned it earlier in the book. Train the pony at home by introducing him to as many unusual situations that you can, safely of course.

Minimus class (jumping)

The minimus involves jumping a course of fences and receiving a rosette if you go clear. Occasionally a show will stretch its funds to a small trophy. The minimus is great for practicing as, when entering the ring, the rider can chose how high the fences will be. The rider can even have the poles on the first hole if they wish. You simply pay your money and have fun in the ring, no pressure.

Ridden Classes

For the child rider there will be two or three classes, starting with the lead rein. The lead rein class will be the first class a small child will enter. It is simple and a kind introduction to the show ring. The child is not alone and will be guided round the ring by his leader (usually parent or similar). The class will usually only include walk and trot. The judge will give an indication of what is required as it will vary from judge to judge. The lead rein is usually for one season only. Occasionally, your child may qualify for two years depending on age. Most shows have an upper age limit for the lead rein. However children as young as three can be seen performing in this class. At this age they appear to do little more than bounce around in the saddle. Having said that, it is a good introduction to showing, I have yet to see a young child in this class without a beaming smile!

For the riding classes the rider should, by this stage of competition, be able to at least walk a straight line and trot a figure of eight. The rider should be working towards the canter figure of eight.

The first ridden class will be the next step up from lead rein. Again this is a simple class and a good introduction to the bigger class. The rider will be required to trot a figure of eight but will not be expected to canter (some riders do if able). The judge will be lenient and encourage the children in the class in order to make it pleasant. The child will do lead rein and first ridden in their first two show seasons.

Jumping classes

The first jumping class a child will do is the lead rein. The parent or guardian will lead the child and pony round a small course while also jumping the fences with the child and pony. This class is very hard work for the leader and the leader must therefore be fit and able. The fences will be very small so that the pony and child gain in confidence before moving to the next classes. This class is usually performed for a season at the very least but again this will depend on age of the child and the rules of the organisers.

The child will advance their jumping in the very smallest and simplest class, that of the nervous/novice or beginners. These classes are for the complete beginner and are a really kind introduction to the real thing. The show organisers should always help the beginners to get around with little pressure as possible on the child. Obviously this class is performed without the leader!

In Hand Classes

Children do seem to love doing in hand classes. In hand classes with a sensible pony are easy and fun to do. The child can of course go in with an adult if need be. During the first few attempts this would be sensible as the class can be daunting to a very young child on their own.

The in hand classes require the child to lead their pony around the ring with all the other competitors in the class. The judge then asks every competitor to line up with their pony. The judge will then call each child and pony out so that he can chat with the handler and then judge the pony as it stands before him.

Once the child has spent the season trying different classes they should begin to have an idea of what discipline they would like to specialise in.

Once the child decides (they may not even want to compete) what it is they want to specialise in you can then purchase the proper attire. Until such time the rider will compete in the hat, jodhpurs and boots that have been worn for lessons. A school blazer/shirt and tie will get the rider through the first season thus preventing any unnecessary outlay.

Whatever the child decides to do it is vital that the riding is always enjoyed first and foremost. With a horse riding career ahead good beginnings are important, especially the way the child treats their pony. I have seen many children sadly abusing ponies in and around the show ring. I urge you to instil care and compassion towards the pony at all times. If you are at a show and see abusive behaviour towards a pony please always report the incident to the show organiser. Ponies deserve love and respect as they give us so much joy and laughter (tears sometimes). The pony deserves to enjoy the times shared with the rider, it is the very least we can do when they serve us so well!

Show days can be long and tiring not just for us but more so for the ponies and horses. Make sure your child or the child you are with does not spend the day galloping around the show ground as many children do. It is unsafe for all concerned. Not only is it unsafe but it is also tiring and unfair for the pony. After a day at a show the pony must rest the next day. If at all possible, a couple of days off would be even more beneficial to the pony.

When planning for the pony's first show you must think about the behaviour he may display. He may not be his usual placid self at a show ground. Some ponies get very excited, especially early on in the season. Just be aware that you will need to be more protective of your child rider than you are perhaps at home. Usually after a couple of shows, the pony should calm down and take the day more in his stride.

Hacking Alone

Allowing a child rider to hack out alone is a very worrying decision. There are many factors to consider in deciding to give them independence on a hack.

- Reliability of the pony
- Types of hacking available in the area
- Traffic volume
- Likely hazards
- Age of the child (13yrs and older are capable of hacking with friends)

It seems that once a child becomes a teenager they want to branch out and meet with friends etc. This of course is understandable and independence needs to be encouraged.

The pony must be bombproof and accept any form of traffic. They must be sensible and able to cope with the many hazards that can appear on a hack. You must know the pony inside out and be sure that he is 100% in all situations.

Possible Hazards to consider

- Traffic including cars, Lorries and motorcycles with the occasional tractor depending on your area.
- Off road motorcycles
- Ramblers (can be equally scary)
- Dogs on and off leads
- Children
- Bicycles
- Joggers
- Farm animals that the pony has not seen before (pigs seem to frighten many equines)

I am sure you can think of others as there are so many different hazards out there. It is a sad state, but motorists are becoming more aggressive towards riders (or anything else that will slow them down). I meet some wonderful motorists don't get me wrong. Some will pull over, slow down and smile! However there is a minority that think it's ok to speed past a group of ponies. You also have a minority that will insist on passing on narrow lanes with just a hairs breath of room between the car and the pony; all this while managing to verbally abuse riders as well. High visibility tabards with instructions on are a good thing to wear. For example *Pass wide and slow*. Again, most drivers oblige, but sadly still the minority exists. The Polite range of fluorescent coats and high visibility clothes are very good. Many drivers think they are police uniforms and this does slow motorists down very well!

I am not having a go at motorists as many are wonderful and sometimes with the ignorance of many riders I can see why motorists get fed up with us. I see it from both angles and riders need to be polite and thank motorists who kindly oblige us!

Tractor drivers are usually very kind and will slow or even stop for riders. Many dog owners will put their dogs on leads as ponies pass them but the odd one still manages to weave bravely in and out of pony legs!

So you need to be sure the pony is 100% bombproof before allowing your child to hack off into the sunset. I would not consider a child hacking alone until they are at the very least a competent teenager. Even then it would be local and not involve a main road. I would need to know their planned route and know how long they would be.

Chapter 8

Giving Something Back to the Pony

This section is especially for the Kids

If we own our pony, or we loan or borrow or hire, we still need to always cherish them as sentient beings. Sentient means that they have feelings. Ponies feel pain, sadness and happiness just like we do. They have their passions; they love and hate the same as we do. They enjoy attention and care just like us too. They are not machines like many riders seem to think.

I have been round ponies for so many years and have seen some terrible abuse. A lot of this abuse has been encouraged by parents. Without parents endorsing abuse then children would not think it was alright to do it.

I have been at many pony shows over the years and been so very sad at what I have seen. Ponies, working so hard for their owners, only to then be thrashed, when things go wrong. Even rider error often brings about a good smack for ponies. I do not want to hark on too much about the horror I have seen but the final chapter of this book will help us put it right.

When things do go wrong it is often not the fault of the pony! In fact, it is very rare to find it is. Generally it is rider error, such as, not making our signals to the pony clear enough. Maybe sometimes we just don't listen to the pony when he signals to us that he is tired, frightened or unsure of what we want him to do. Maybe he just feels sore somewhere in his back or legs and we just don't care enough to notice!

It is important that, at the end of the day, we give something back to our pony in order that they will feel appreciated and loved. Ponies like attention and love and this will be evident when you put into practice some of the ideas I am about to put forward.

Always, always, gently caress your pony when he has done something really good for you. This is a very basic reward system that should be the very least you do by habit each time you ride. The sound of a chirpy voice as you stroke his neck will tell the pony that you are pleased with him.

When riding your pony, always make sure that you get into the habit of listening to what the pony has to say. Of course he cannot talk to you using language that we do. But he will use body language and you as the rider need to know a little bit about the subject.

If your pony is usually well behaved and begins to be naughty when you are riding him, this could be his way of telling you he is hurting. If he usually stands at the mounting block when you get on, but suddenly starts getting agitated, he could be trying to tell you his back is sore. If your pony behaves differently in any way ask yourself why?

Other signs of pain to look for

- Ears back
- Pony refusing to be caught
- Pony hiding in the back of the stable

- Pony dipping his back as you mount
- Grinding teeth
- Tossing head a lot
- Change in head carriage
- Swishing of the tail
- Bucking
- Rearing

The above are subtle signs that you will need to take notice of. The more obvious sign of pain is lameness but that will show itself readily with a limping pony.

I am not sure who told me the philosophy I now live by with my horses, but it has always served me well to this very day. "Walk the first and last five minutes and your horse will keep well."

I have always warmed up and cooled down well and I have never had any problems with my many horses to date.

Massage and Touch

Ponies love to be massaged and touched in a gentle calming manner. Massage can make a pony feel very relaxed and very special. I have seen it so many times over the years.

Why Massage?

We massage because it does the pony good. It relaxes all the muscles and improves the circulation of the pony. It also helps bring about a deeper bond between you and your pony. You will notice during a massage session that your pony will probably fall asleep as you work on him. You may see other wonderful reactions, such as:

- Twitching of the muzzle area
- Drooping of the eyes
- Sighing
- Resting a limb
- Stretching
- Head making its way to the floor

It is a wonderful feeling when you see your pony enjoying something so much. It is a way to say thank you for all he does for you.

How do I massage my Pony?

You do not have to be specially qualified to massage your pony. If you have the intent inside you, then just the act of stroking him with your hands will be a start.

Make sure you are wearing your hard hat for safety around your pony. Tie the pony in a quiet place using a quick release knot, as always. Talk gently to the pony as you begin to stroke him with the flat of your hand all the way down his neck. Continue stroking from the top of his neck to the base for around five minutes. Then stroke with the flat of your hand along his back and ribs. Perform this for around five minutes also. Then move to his hind quarter muscles and perform the same. Once you have finished move onto the opposite side of the pony and start again.

Next take a gentle hold on a clump of mane and run your fingers from the top of the hair to the bottom. Also with the same small clump hold at the root and rotate clockwise and anticlockwise a couple of times each. Perform this from the top of the mane to the base. Perform the same exercise with the forelock.

Linda Tellington-Jones has written a lovely book full of ideas for massage and calming things to do for your pony. The next exercise is my favourite from her book and makes my ponies calm and sleepy and oh so relaxed.

Stand at the side of your pony and place your left or right hand, depending which is more comfortable, on your pony. With the finger tops in contact with your pony move the fingers in a circle, the length of your hand, around a full circle and a quarter. Start at the position of six thirty and rotate until you have done a full hour and then a quarter of the clock face. This will mean you finish at the position of six forty five. This can be performed over each side of the pony from top to bottom.

How Long do I Massage my Pony?

There are no rules to the length of time you can massage your pony. Even five minutes a day is good and will make your pony feel good. On the other hand, if you have lots of time and can do half an hour occasionally, that is wonderful. You will find it difficult to do much longer that half an hour as it is rather demanding work.

Another simple gift for your pony is time. Slip on a headcollar and lead him out onto some fresh grass. This can be around the stables where you keep him (make sure you ask the yard owner or farmer). If safe to do so, you could lead him out onto the surrounding grass verges, check with mum and dad first, it may even be nice if they went with you to make sure you were safe. The pony will enjoy you spending special time with him. A time when you are not riding him but just being with him.

The above ideas are just suggestions. There are so many things you can do with your pony other than riding him. Sit and watch him in his paddock. You can learn so much just by observing your pony with his field companions. This will be nice relaxing time for you too. You will become closer to your pony and a strong bond will should develop over a short period of time.

HAPPY RIDING

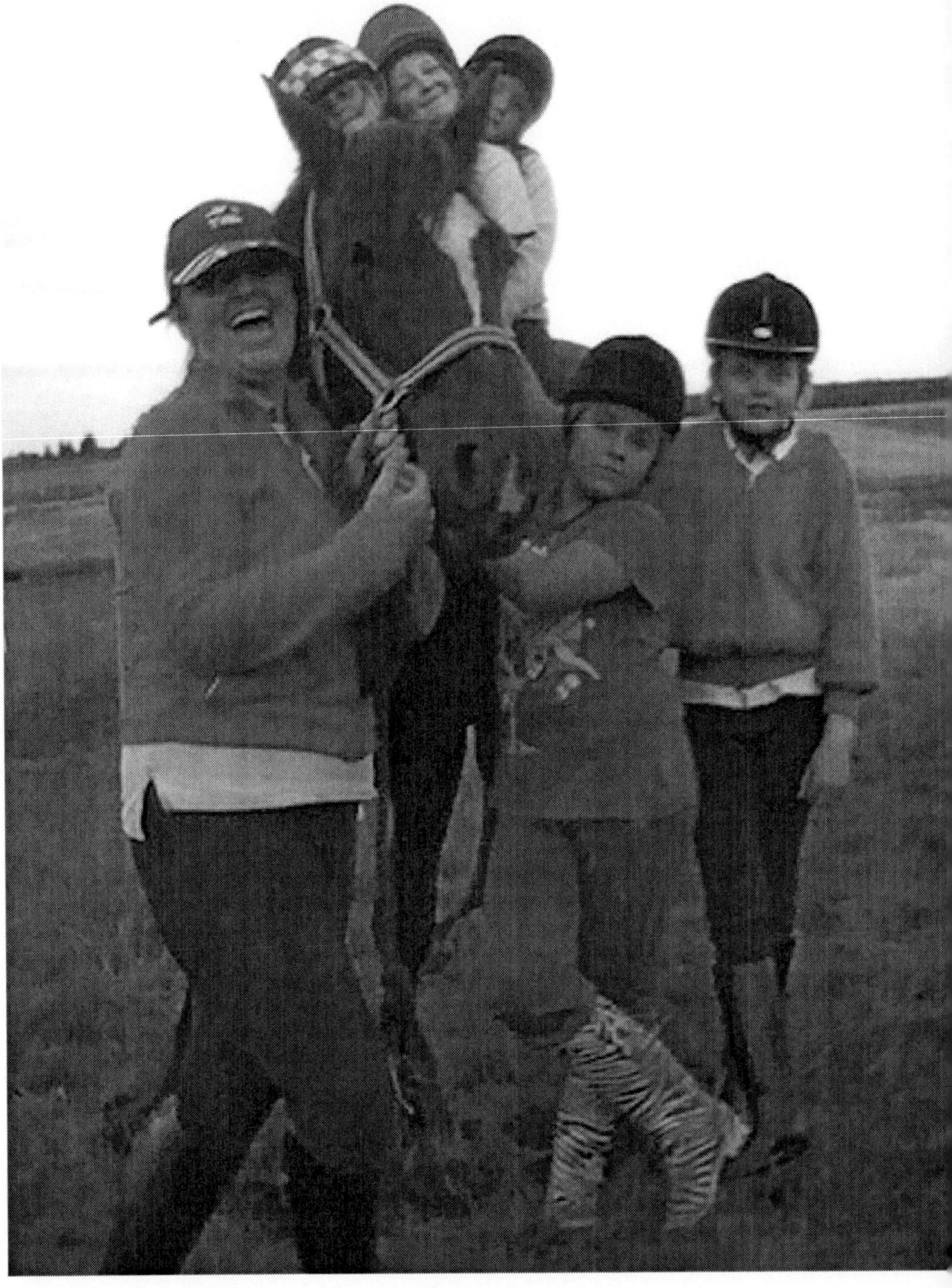

Published in 2013 by FeedARead.com Publishing – Arts Council funded

Copyright © The author as named on the book cover.

First Edition

The author has asserted their moral right under the Copyright, Designs and Patents Act, 1988, to be identified as the author of this work.

All Rights reserved. No part of this publication may be reproduced, copied, stored in a retrieval system, or transmitted, in any form or by any means, without the prior written consent of the copyright holder, nor be otherwise circulated in any form of binding or cover other than that in which it is published and without a similar condition being imposed on the subsequent purchaser.

A CIP catalogue record for this title is available from the British Library.

Lightning Source UK Ltd.
Milton Keynes UK
UKOW02f0236040616

275582UK00001B/224/P

9 781782 993780